Year 6

Written by
Katherine McFarlane

Illustrated by
Luke Jurevicius

Sequential spelling strategies in context.

Pascal Press

This book belongs to

____

Pascal Press
PO Box 250
Glebe NSW Australia 2037
Ph: (02) 8585 4044
http://www.pascalpress.com.au

Reprinted 1999, 2002, 2003, 2005, 2007, 2011 (twice)

ISBN 978 186441 264 2

Series editor: Sharon Shapiro
Designed by Love of Design Electronic Publishing
Typeset by Artwork Express
Printed by Green Giant Press

Introduction

Spelling Works! is a structured spelling program for children in years 3 - 6. It contains sequential and consistently developed spelling activities. Within each book, strategies and skills are introduced and then reinforced in later units. Students become familiar with the most frequently used words while also developing strategies for spelling new words. A teacher can use **Spelling Works!** as the basis of a thorough spelling programme.

This book focuses on the major strategies including spelling rules, word families, syllabification, proof reading, visual memory, word building and analogy. It includes work on using a dictionary and exercises on blends, compound words, contractions and homophones.

Spelling Works! also includes a program of exercises in word study and correct usage. When writing, students have to make many decisions that involve choosing base words, adding prefixes and suffixes and then spelling them correctly to create sentences that makes sense. Knowing and using the grammatical parts of speech, writing sentences, using punctuation and building on base words are all an integral part of creating meaningful texts.

The structure of this book

This book has 32 double page units. The left page introduces new concepts or rules while the right page reinforces concepts. That means the left page is suitable for classroom use while the right could be used as part of a homework program.

For each term there are eight units plus a review. The second page of each unit has a text that uses list words in context. These linked texts use a variety of writing styles to add interest and make spelling an integrated part of your English program.

Term reviews allow teachers to ascertain whether concepts have been grasped.

To cater for the different abilities within a classroom there are basic lists and extension words in each unit. Room has been left for children to add their own words and challenge activities are included in each unit.

Answers to all activities are provided in an eight page lift-out section.

The dictionary included in each book is a simple, easy to use reference that allows students to work independently.

Spelling rules – a quick guide, appears at the back of this book.

CONTENTS

CONTENTS

EASY SKILLS REFERENCE

Content	Pages where exercises are located
Abbreviations/Contractions	37, 39, 41, 43, 48, 51, 55, 64, 65, 68
Adjectives	6, 7, 10, 11, 13, 21, 31, 32, 48, 62, 66, 69
Adverbs	27, 69
Anagrams	2, 6
Analogies	38, 50, 56, 58, 60, 62
Antonyms	4, 5, 8, 10, 30, 32, 38, 48, 62
Blends	23, 50
Clauses	45, 47, 49, 55, 59, 64, 67, 69
Conjunctions	34, 37, 39, 41, 57
Crosswords	8, 32, 70
Degrees of comparison	21, 42, 43
Dictionary work	3, 31, 38, 42, 44, 52, 56, 60, 62, 64, 65, 66
Direct/Indirect speech	25, 29, 47, 61
Extension words	2, 5, 8, 10, 15, 19, 22, 24, 25, 28, 34, 38, 40, 42, 44, 46, 48, 52, 60, 62, 63, 66, 68, 70
Gender	27
Homophones	1, 6, 22, 23, 32, 43, 50, 56
Idioms	4, 16, 21, 22, 34, 42, 46, 52, 64, 66, 68, 70
List word exercises	2, 4, 13, 19, 22, 24, 25, 32, 33, 41, 44, 46, 52, 58, 62, 63, 68, 70
Nouns	1, 3, 4, 13, 20, 23, 34, 40, 44, 59
Occupations	10, 14, 58
Phrases	25, 37, 39, 41, 46, 47, 55, 69
Plurals	1, 3, 5, 7, 9, 11, 19, 29, 61, 62
Prefixes	3, 5, 8, 13, 14, 15, 21, 25, 27, 31, 40, 45, 50, 51, 55, 57, 58, 60, 61, 63, 69
Pronouns	9, 16
Proof reading	2, 6, 14, 15, 20, 24, 33, 37, 39, 42, 46, 51, 56, 60, 63, 68, 69, 70
Proverbs	24, 26, 28, 30, 40, 44, 48
Relative pronouns	31, 44
Sentence study	4, 52
Similes	59
Suffixes	3, 6, 7, 8, 9, 11, 14, 15, 21, 23, 27, 28, 40, 43, 47, 49, 50, 55, 66, 67
Syllables	63
Synonyms	16, 20, 24, 43, 55, 70
Thesaurus	26, 28, 41, 59, 64, 68
Verbs	5, 7, 12, 15, 19, 33, 43, 48, 55, 61, 65, 69
Vocabulary	8, 10, 11, 12, 13, 14, 16, 19, 20, 22, 23, 25, 28, 29, 30, 34, 38, 48, 49, 50, 52, 60, 64, 66, 67, 68
Word building	9, 16, 23, 31, 69

How to study a word

1 **LOOK** at the whole word.

What does it mean?

excessive

2 **SAY** the word slowly.

How many syl/la/bles are there?

3 **STUDY** the word.

excessive

What is the difficult part?
Do you know other words with this pattern?
Close your eyes.
Can you see the word?
Write the word in the air.

4 **WRITE** the word from memory.

Write each part.
Don't say the letter names.

5 **CHECK** the word.

Were you right?
If not, try again.

UNIT 1 Extension

accept	ankle
ascent	apply
article	battle
bandage	carriage
panic	vast
gaze	habit
harvest	haste

acceptable
acceptance
application
applicant
applicable
battled
panicked
vastness
vastly
habitual
____
____

1. LOOKING AT NOUNS

Nouns are the names of people, animals, ideas, places, things and feelings.

Write the nouns in the first two sentence of the text.

a. ____________________________________
____

Common nouns name common things.

e.g. dog, cat, road, house

Underline the common nouns.

b. The injured boy gazed in panic at his twisted ankle.

c. The gold rush caused many problems.

Proper nouns are the names of particular people, animals, places and things.

e.g. Cindy, Boundary Road, Anzac Day

Underline the proper nouns.

d. Amanda, Tegan and Leah went to the Jenolan Caves last Thursday.

e. Mr Truscott travelled to Wagga Wagga.

2. WORD STUDY

Many singular words add 's' to form plurals. Words that end with 's', 'ch', 'sh', 'x' or 'z' add 'es'.

e.g. box — boxes
virus — viruses

Write the plural.

a. ditch ____________
b. climax ____________
c. brush ____________
d. mattress ____________
e. buzz ____________

Find antonyms (opposites) in the list words.

f. offer ____________
g. descent ____________
h. calm ____________
i. small ____________

Add each prefix and suffix to 'apply'.

re	s	ed	ing

j. ____________ ____________
____________ ____________

3. Select-A-WORD

a. They all went to the party __________ for Larissa. (accept, except)

b. He did not wait around to __________ the prize. (accept, except)

c. The group will __________ the mountain in the morning. (ascent, ascend)

d. Will the __________ of the north face be attempted early? (ascent, ascend)

Circle the word that does not belong.

e. carriage, trailer, truck, engine

PART 1

The Eureka Stockade

Gold was discovered in Victoria in 1854. In haste new settlers rushed to find their fortunes. Across vast tracts of country the miners came by horse, carriage and on foot. Gold fever caused scenes of panic at the diggings.

The gold rush caused a number of problems. There was a great increase in population and it was difficult for the authorities to control lawless behaviour.

Each miner had to apply for a $3 per month licence permitting him to dig for gold. (This would be equivalent to $100 in today's money!). This fee had to be paid each month even if the miner found no gold. This was difficult to accept.

Among the miners were many men interested in a democratic form of government, which would give them more rights.

... continued on Page 2

5. CORNER Challenge

Choose extension words.

a. The __________ form was completed by the new arrival.

b. Josie was an __________ for the position of receptionist.

c. The visitors admired the sheer beauty and the __________ of the mountain region.

Find 2 words to complete the word cross.

d.

			D			

4. word usage

Choose list words.

a. Kylie was happy to __________ the prize.

b. Did you __________ for a driver's licence?

c. The wooden __________ had been stored for many years.

d. Across the __________ plain the animals roamed.

e. When it came to __________ time, all the farmers were very busy.

f. When the bell rang they came in __________ to the new building.

6. Proof Reading

Underline the incorrectly spelt words and rewrite below.

a. They began the asent of the mountin at eight o'clock.

b. Were the articels placed in the carrage?

____

____

Anagram. Movement by a horse: 'trance' __________

UNIT 2 Extension

imagine	immediate
incident	imaginary
bitumen	independent
fiction	interesting
figure	library
liquid	tight
rifle	twist

imagination
incidental
independence
disinterested
fictitious
fictional
figurine
librarian
liquify
liquified
rifling

____

____

1. LOOKING AT nouns

Nouns that name things that exist in our ideas and feelings are called abstract nouns.

e.g. sadness, love, bravery

Underline the abstract nouns.

a. Looks of astonishment and dismay could be seen on their faces.

b. A feeling of sadness and despair was noticed in the family.

Form abstract nouns from the bracketed words.

c. My ___________ (friend) with Jim has grown over ten years.

d. The ___________ (wise) of the old man was respected by all.

e. His ___________ (honest) was valued.

Add 'ian' to form common nouns.

f. one who deals with magic ___________

g. one who plays or composes music ___________

2. WORD STUDY

If a word ends with a consonant and a 'y', the 'y' is changed to an 'i' and 'es' is added to the plural.

e.g. library — libraries

Write the plural.

a. city ___________

b. territory ___________

c. injury ___________

d. comedy ___________

Add prefixes and suffixes to the base word. Use the words in the sentences below.

(un) imagine

es	ed	ing	ative	ation	ary

e. ______________________________

____

____

f. She won first prize with the very ___________ poem she wrote.

g. By using his ___________ he solved the complex problem.

h. The equator is an ___________ line running around the earth.

3. Dictionary Work

Circle the words that would be first in a dictionary.

a. imbalance, immaterial, immediate, immigrate

b. instrument, incident, instantly, insurance

Arrange in alphabetical order.

c. Tonya, Hayna, Shazia, Shunling, Tai, Nadiya, Chiraasi, Elise, Howard, Jennet, Sherin

____

____

____

____

PART 2

The Eureka Stockade

The miners wanted <u>immediate</u> changes – an abolished or reduced licence fee and the right to vote.

The governor at the time, Governor Latrobe, reduced the licence fee to $4 for three months. Latrobe was replaced by Governor Hotham, and an important <u>incident</u> took place.

At Ballarat a miner was killed, and the local hotel keeper was accused of the murder. He was tried and acquitted. The miners were upset and <u>rifle</u> shots were heard in the main street. The miners rioted and the hotel was burnt. The hotel keeper, Bentley, was tried again, found guilty and sentenced to three years in jail.

The Ballarat Reform League was set up, and after many <u>interesting</u> meetings, demanded the abolition of licence fees, votes for every man, frequent elections and payment for elected representatives. A leading <u>figure</u> in the events was a miner, Peter Lalor.

... continued on Page 4

5. CORNER Challenge

Name this group or collection.

a. __________ of stars

b. __________ of grapevines

c. __________ of furniture

d. __________ of poems

e. __________ of scones

f. __________ of people in church

Write these verbs as nouns.

Hint: Write '**the**' before and '**of**' after.
behave —
(the) behaviour (of)

g. necessary __________

h. anxious __________

i. savage __________

j. remain __________

k. suggest __________

4. LOOKING AT statements and questions

Simple sentences have a verb and express a complete thought. Simple sentences can be statements or questions.

Add suitable verbs. Check whether each sentence is a statement (S) or question (Q).

a. They __________ the gear from the sports room. ❑ S ❑ Q

b. My older brother __________ some of them. ❑ S ❑ Q

c. __________ you __________ the trail across the mountain? ❑ S ❑ Q

6. Select-A-WORD

Select a list word.

a. The delicate porcelain __________ was placed on display.

b. The workers made an __________ start at seven o'clock.

c. The __________ creature was drawn on the wall.

d. All the __________ in the flask was spilt.

Find antonyms in the list.

e. dull __________ f. fact __________

g. loose __________ h. real __________

Sayings. Explain 'To shed crocodile tears' __________

UNIT 3 Extension

bore	border
borrow	forth
mobile	towel
tongue	solar
sword	rocket
soldier	correct
co-operate	worship

boring
borrower
forthwith
mobility
mobilise
mobilization
rocketry
incorrect
correction
co-operatively
____
____

1. LOOKING AT verbs

Verbs tell us what something is or what is being done. There are action (e.g. ran)**, thinking** (e.g. forgot)**, feeling** (e.g. hated)**, saying** (e.g. shouted) **and linking** (e.g. is) **verbs.**

Write the verbs in the first two sentences of the text.

a. ____________________________
____

Use these compound verbs in sentences.

b. will be co-operating
____
____

c. may have bored
____
____

Add compound verbs.

d. The towel ________________ on the wall for days.

e. The soldiers ________________ towards the camp yesterday.

f. ________ Sheila ________ the glasses on the tray?

2. WORD STUDY

Singular nouns ending with a vowel and 'y' add 's' to form the plural.

e.g. survey — surveys

a. chimney ____________
b. storey ____________
c. quay ____________
d. volley ____________

Find antonyms in the list.

e. wrong ____________
f. stationary ____________
g. entertain ____________
h. loan ____________

Add prefixes 'in', 'il' and 'ir' to form antonyms.

e.g. incorrect — not correct

i. ____________ not regular
j. ____________ not sincere
k. ____________ against the law
l. ____________ not able to be read

3. Using Extension Words

a. He was the ____________ of a large sum of money.

b. The ____________ of the armed forces needed to be quick.

c. The students worked ____________ on the project.

d. They were told to start the work ____________.

e. Because she did not have ____________ in her injured arm, she could not enter the event.

Build the word family for 'mobile'.

f. ____________________
____
____

PART 3

The Eureka Stockade

The miners found it impossible to co-operate with the authorities. A meeting was held at the border of Walleneep Gully.

The miners built a stockade and hoped to defeat the government forces or make them agree to their demands. A flag, the Southern Cross, became a symbol of their struggle.

Peter Lalor, their leader, and his followers captured Government arms and ammunition. They declared the 'Republic of Victoria'.

On the 4th December, 1884 three hundred soldiers marched forth and quickly defeated the miners. Thirty miners and five soldiers were killed. The ring leaders of the revolt and one hundred and twenty-five miners were captured.

The authorities set up a commission to enquire into their complaints. Licence fees were abolished and replaced by a 'Miners Right' costing $2 per year. The miners were granted the right to vote.

4. word usage

Add suffixes.

a. The machine was (bore) __________ into the rock face.

b. Have all the items been (borrow) __________ from the shed?

c. The new houses were built (border) __________ the National Park.

d. The people (worship) __________ at the local church.

e. The (co-operative) __________ of all the people in the village was needed.

5. CORNER Challenge

Add words.

a.

V					D
S					G

Form adjectives (describing words) from these words.

e.g. anger — angry

b. action __________

c. object __________

d. progress __________

e. cease __________

Select the correct word.

f. She had been a __________ in the house for several years. (border, boarder)

g. The wild __________ charged into the scrub. (bore, boar)

6. Proof Reading

Rewrite incorrectly spelt words.

Close to the boarder, the soldir drank his forth bottle of water while wiping his face with the borowed towl.

____

____

Anagram. Form a word meaning worthiness from 'timer' __________

UNIT 4 Extension

secret	section
select	serious
service	several
senator	secretary
sign	silence
silent	similar
simple	sincerely

secretive
dissection
seriously
serviceable
signature
silently
dissimilar
similarity
simplify
insincerity
____
____

1. LOOKING AT verbs

Compound verbs are made up of a main verb and an auxiliary verb.

e.g. She had simplified the work.
auxiliary (had) *main* (simplified)

List the verbs in the first three sentences of the text. Circle the main verbs.

a. ________________________________
____

Verbs can be written in the present tense (now), **past tense** (yesterday) **or future tense** (tomorrow).

Identify the tense of each verb.

b. ________ She will take the book home.
c. ________ The signature was written in the book.
d. ________ The youth is setting up the sign.

Compound verbs can have present or past participles.

e.g. She has signed. *(past)*
She is signing. *(present)*

Write the present and past participles.

e. select __________ __________
f. throw __________ __________

2. WORD STUDY

Words ending with 'f' or 'fe' change their endings to 'ves' to form plurals.

Write the plurals.

a. half __________
b. wharf __________
c. thief __________
d. yourself __________

The suffixes 'able' and 'ible' mean *capable of*.

e.g. serviceable
— capable of being used

e. __________ capable of being unhappy
f. __________ capable of being heard
g. __________ able to be eaten
h. __________ capable of being seen

3. word usage

Adjectives are describing words telling us *how many, how much* and *what kind*.

Complete using a list word and adjective.

a. A __________ __________ of the building was repaired after the cyclone.
b. The people were impressed by the __________ __________ at the new hotel.
c. The __________ __________ made a speech in parliament.
d. The __________ __________ was able to complete all the office work.

PART 1

Water in Australia

Oceans, seas, lakes and rivers cover almost three-quarters of the surface of the earth. All life on earth depends on water, and most living things are largely made up of water. About two-thirds of our body and about nine-tenths of our blood consist of water. In a year, you take in about a tonne of water by simply drinking and eating foods.

On a map of Australia, you will notice select areas that are well supplied with rivers and streams. There are other large areas of central and southern Australia that do not have a river system and have frequent serious water shortages. These areas often have several rivers that only flow over short sections after it rains.

Australia's main river system consists of the Murray, Darling and Murrumbidgee Rivers in the south-eastern part of the continent. These three rivers drain an area similar in size to France.

... continued on Page 10

5. CORNER Challenge

Complete the crossword puzzle.

a.		W								
b.				C	I					
c.	B									
d.								A	T	E
e.			P	P						
f.				L	I					
g.			A	S	C					
h.	S									
i.			A							
j.			D							

a. to pay homage to
b. a happening or event
c. a type of road surface
d. to work well with others
e. putting to practical use
f. a fluid
g. the climb up a slope
h. part of something
i. done in haste
j. removing the moisture

4. Select-A-WORD

Find antonyms in the list.

a. well-known ____________

b. humorous ____________

c. noise ____________

Add suffixes to 'sign' and 'simple' to complete the sentences.

d. It was difficult to read the ____________ at the bottom of the form.

e. He had to ____________ the work so that everyone could do it.

6. Using Extension Words

a. The soldier was ____________ wounded in the battle.

b. Do you think that this old machine is still ____________?

c. The animals moved ____________ through the thick grass.

d. Because she was such a ____________ person no one knew much about her.

Clothing. a. Who would wear a fez? ____________ b. Who wears a busby? ____________

UNIT 5 Extension

budget	burglar
human	public
puncture	purchase
purpose	curtain
nuclear	numerous
vacuum	musician
unique	usable

budgeting
humane
inhumanity
publicity
publication
purchasing
purposely
musical
uniquely
reusable

____

____

1. LOOKING AT pronouns

Pronouns are used in place of nouns.

e.g. He said that they had taken a good supply of water with them.

Underline the pronouns.

a. She waited with her sister for all their brothers to arrive.

b. Have you ever seen how it will float on the water?

c. My elder sister came with us when we went to their home.

d. When will you give the book to me?

e. Our friends from Sweden will be staying with us when they arrive.

Use these pair of pronouns in sentences.

f. | they | themselves | ________________

____

____

g. | my | it | ________________________

____

____

2. WORD STUDY

Singular words ending in 'o' usually add 'es' to form the plural.

e.g. cargo — cargoes

Write the plurals.

a. buffalo ____________

b. potato ____________

c. volcano ____________

d. tomato ____________

If there is a vowel before the 'o' add 's' to form the plural. Words related to music also simply add 's'.

Write the plurals.

e. rodeo ____________

f. solo ____________

g. trio ____________

h. radio ____________

The suffixes 'ar', 'er', 'or' mean *one who*.

e.g. burglar — one who steals from homes

Write the words that mean:

i. one who manages a business

____

j. one who buys regularly

____

k. one who carries luggage

____

l. one who sells fruit __________

3. Select-A-WORD

Choose built 'use' words to complete.

a. The old house had remained __________ for many years.

b. This very __________ appliance has worked over ten years.

c. She discarded the old __________ pieces of material.

d. All the workers were __________ employed finishing the work.

Water in Australia PART 2

Australia has many large lakes that are shallow, salty and often dry. The largest of these is Lake Eyre, which lies below sea level in the central basin. For most of the year, it is a dried-up salt flat, because the rivers that feed it flow only after rain.

Australia has, however, a large underground lake, called the Great Artesian Basin, which is below a large area of the plains and deserts. The excess rainfall in eastern Queensland seeps through the porous limestone rock and is stored in this immense artesian basin. <u>Numerous</u> flowing bores tap this huge underground water storage system, and supply water for sheep and cattle stations. <u>Human</u> settlement would have been impossible without this <u>usable</u> source.

Desert land covers about two-fifths of our continent. This dry region is the second largest desert area in the world. Only the Sahara Desert of North Africa is larger.

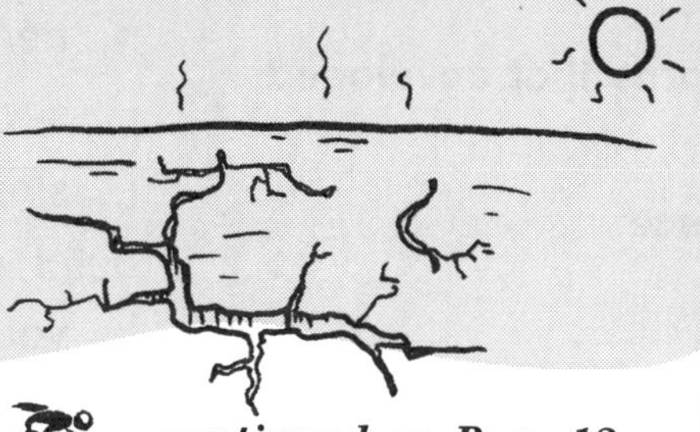

... continued on Page 12

5. CORNER Challenge

Find words for the spaces.

a.

P	U	N	C	T	U	R	E	D

RAT words.

b. one who is a member of royalty or the nobility ____________

c. the dictator of a country ____________

d. one who believes in government by the people ____________

Choose adjectives for these words.

e. budget ____________

f. ____________ puncture

g. ____________ purchase

4. word usage

Choose antonyms from the list.

a. private ____________ b. sell ____________

c. common ____________ d. scarce ____________

Use antonyms of list words to complete.

e. The ____________ meeting was held in the house across the road.

f. ____________ animals were moving down the road at dusk.

g. This is a very ____________ object found in almost every home.

h. The ____________ material from the construction site was disposed of yesterday.

6. Using Extension Words

a. well-illustrated ____________

b. interesting ____________ event

c. ____________ carefully for a new car

d. ____________ plastic containers

Use in a sentence.

e. | budgeting | unique |

____

____

Occupations. Explain: stevedore ________________________________

UNIT 6 Extension

boundary	cough
council	youth
tourist	thoroughly
ruin	guilt
built	guide
juicy	suitable
soak	contribution

boundaries
councillor
youthful
tourism
thoroughness
ruination
guilty
guiltily
juiciness
suitability
____
____

1. LOOKING AT *language*

Many English words have root words that developed from a Latin word.

The Latin root 'pono' means 'I place'.

These words derived:
opponent, depot, preposition, impostor, compose, dispose, deposit, opposite.

Match these words to their meanings.

a. __________ a place for storage
b. __________ one who takes another person's place
c. __________ to put together in writing
d. __________ a word which goes before a group of words
e. __________ one who is against another person
f. __________ to place away, to discard

The Latin root 'decem' means 'ten'.
Find four words which have been derived from it.

g. __________ __________
__________ __________

2. WORD STUDY

The suffix 'ion' means 'the act of'.
e.g. ruination — the act of reducing to ruins

The suffix 'ness' means the 'state of being'.
e.g. thoroughness — state of being complete

Add suffixes 'ion' or 'ness'.

a. contribute __________
b. attract __________
c. weary __________
d. bright __________

Write these words.

e. __________ state of being happy
f. __________ state of taking care
g. __________ the act of allowing

Write as plurals.

h. hero __________
i. success __________
j. stretch __________

Build into adjectives.

k. youth __________
l. ruin __________
m. guilt __________

3. Vocabulary

Circle the more suitable word.

a. The warring nations will bring their argument/dispute to the United Nations.
b. The coach was due to depart/leave at five o'clock.
c. The officer was pleased to have the opportunity/chance to discuss the problem.
d. The decorator inspected the inside/interior of the building.
e. The rescued sailor was very thankful/grateful for the help.

PART 3

Water in Australia

Water suitable for domestic use, industry and farming is stored in dams, reservoirs, weirs, levees and lakes. Lake Burley Griffin in Canberra is a fine example of a man-made lake.

Pure water is a colourless, tasteless liquid. It is a compound made up of two gases, hydrogen and oxygen. The water held in our water storage areas is not completely pure. It usually contains minerals dissolved from the surrounding soil, particles of soil and decaying vegetation and, often, bacteria which can cause diseases. This water is not always safe for drinking and must be treated with chemicals to purify it thoroughly.

Water is truly the life blood of our land. We must use it wisely and conserve it where possible.

4. word usage

Add a verb and list word.

a. All of the local representatives __________ the c__________ in the hall.

b. The __________ __________ the coach trip to the castles of South Wales.

c. That experienced __________ __________ with us to show us the mountain waterfalls.

d. Do you __________ you could collect a __________ magazine for me to read on the aircraft?

e. The y__________ __________ his new racing bike in the sprint event.

5. CORNER Challenge

The Latin root 'duco' means 'to lead'.

Complete the part words and write them in the sentences.

a. _____duct____

b. _____duct___

c. __duca______

d. ___duct____

e. The famous __________ was in charge of the orchestra.

f. The __________ that he received at the school in Victoria helped him make good progress.

g. This company is famous for the __________ of woollen garments.

h. They were told there was to be a __________ in the hours of overtime worked.

6. Select-A-WORD

though	thought	thorough

a. I __________ that I saw him by the creek.

b. __________ he was very sick, he still completed his work.

c. She tried to be __________ in cleaning the machine.

Famous people. What was named after?

a. James Watt ____________________ b. Louis Pasteur ____________________

UNIT 7

succeed	suffer
surprise	sufficient
substance	subtract
defence	desire
determine	definite
dessert	science
scramble	scientist

Extension

unsuccessful
insufferable
surprising
substantial
defensive
undesirable
determination
indefinitely
unscientific
scientifically

____

____

1. LOOKING AT language

The Latin root 'mitto' means 'I send'.

transmit	emit	dismiss	missile

Select words.

a. The machine will __________ a clicking noise every few minutes.

b. The company will __________ the employee who is always late.

c. They decided to __________ the information to the other firm.

d. The __________ travelled towards the target.

In Latin 'curro' means 'I run'.

e.g. A courier was a runner with a message.

cursory	corridor	recur

Select words.

e. They walked along the narrow __________ of the building.

f. She gave a __________ glance at the broken statue.

2. WORD STUDY

The prefixes 'sub', 'suc', 'sup', 'sug' and 'sus' all mean under.

e.g. subway — under a normal roadway

Connect words and meanings.

submarine
suppress
submerge
suspend
submit

a. to go under the water

b. to surrender oneself to control

c. that which goes under the ocean

d. to press or force under

e. to hang up

Choose list words.

f. to take from

____

g. to be in distress or pain

____

Change to adjectives.

h. succeed __________

i. substance __________

j. defence __________

k. desire __________

3. Vocabulary

Describe these buildings.

a. apartment __________

____

b. kiosk __________

____

c. auditorium __________

____

d. marquee __________

____

e. lodge __________

____

PART 1

Elizabeth – Children's Friend

On 20 September 1886, Elizabeth Kenny was born in northern New South Wales. Shortly after, the family moved to a property on the Darling Downs.

Elizabeth's life on their property was happy and adventurous. She loved horses and spent hours riding in the paddocks near the homestead. One day she had the misfortune to fracture her wrist badly in a fall. She suffered pain and was taken to Toowoomba. On examining the fracture the Doctor said that she must stay in town for treatment. Elizabeth was not happy being left in hospital. The Doctor suggested that Elizabeth stay with him and his wife.

Elizabeth read some books to pass the time. One dealt with the muscle structure of the body. Elizabeth studied it carefully. When she returned home she was interested in helping her younger, weak brother. Elizabeth had sufficient time to work out a series of exercises to strengthen his body. She knew that she wanted to work in medical science and wanted to succeed as a trained nurse.

... continued on Page 16

5. CORNER Challenge

Another Latin root is 'specio' which means 'I see'.

Complete the part words and write them in the sentences.

a. _____spec_____

b. spec________

c. spec__________

d. ___spec__

e. The opening ceremony at the sports event was a great __________

f. Many of the __________ at the football match started cheering.

g. That person is a __________ in the investigation.

h. The old __________ had been searching for gold for several years.

4. word usage

Add prefixes and suffixes to underlined words.

a. A substant____ number of items remained on the shelf.

b. Because the work was ____scientif______ the results were not accepted.

c. Because of her great determin______ she managed to complete the work on time.

d. The subtract______ of the number from one million was too difficult for the child.

6. Proof Reading

Rewrite adding punctuation and correcting spelling mistakes.

the scintist was determinned to collect suficient scintific data so that he could definitly defend his theses.

____

____

____

Occupations. Explain 'a philatelist' ______________________________

UNIT 8 Extension

affection	attention
attraction	competition
direction	conversation
exhibition	introduction
operation	occupation
opposition	permission
procession	publication

affectionately
inattentive
competitively
introductory
occupier
unoccupied
operational
opposing
permissible
publicly
____
____

1. LOOKING AT punctuation

Capital letters are used for names of books, poems, people, places, streets, rivers, oceans, mountains, days and months.

Circle the letters that should be capitals and add full stops, commas and question marks.

a. has your brother craig read the book the sheltered cove by alan rawson

b. meg tejan and cheryn went to maitland last july

c. does jessica hsieh live in canyan road harrisville

d. the countries of great britain are england wales scotland and ireland

Add quotation marks around spoken words.

e. have the laird brothers ever been to bega on the southern coast of new south wales asked ellen

f. i do not know exactly where it has gone the boy said clearly

2. WORD STUDY

The suffix 'ion' forms nouns meaning 'the act of'.

Choose 'ion' words.

caution	affection	extension
contribution	occasion	

a. The __________ to the building took several months to finish.

b. They made a __________ to the local charities' appeal.

c. On that __________ several of the climbers were stranded on the mountain overnight.

d. The boy displayed a great deal of __________ towards his pet cats.

e. They will proceed with __________ along the rough track.

Write as verbs.

f. attention __________

g. procession __________

h. operation __________

i. exhibition __________

3. Using Extension Words

a. The old sea captain was __________ known as 'Ned'.

b. After the speaker's __________ talk the group went to morning tea.

c. The __________ of that building has been there for seven years.

d. The __________ teams ran out onto the field.

Elizabeth – Children's Friend

PART 2

In most countries there are very few cases of infantile paralysis or poliomyelitis because of the great advances in knowledge about the cause and <u>prevention</u> of this terrible disease.

When Elizabeth, now a trained nurse, was twenty-three years old, the disease first came to her <u>attention</u>.

A stockman asked her to come to his house to help his little daughter. On arriving at the house Sister Kenny found a young girl twisting and turning in pain. The Doctor advised her that there was no sure treatment or <u>operation</u> for the disease. After the <u>conversation</u> she was still puzzled.

Sister Kenny noticed that the girl was trying to stop the muscles in her legs contracting. Elizabeth realised that something was needed to help relax the muscles. She tore up a woollen blanket, dipped the strips into hot water and wrapped them around the little girl's legs. Soon the girl fell asleep.

After further treatment, the girl recovered.

... continued on Page 20

5. CORNER Challenge

Explain their meanings.

a. recitation ______________

b. sermon ______________

c. address ______________

d. speech ______________

e. lecture ______________

Use one of these word in a sentence.

f. ______________

4. word usage

Add a verb form from the list.

a. All of the children in the class __________ in the cross country event.

b. The people at the party were __________ to their local member of parliament.

c. The boy will not be __________ to go on the excursion next week.

d. The protesters will __________ down the main street to City Hall.

6. Pronouns

Replace the underlined words with pronouns.

a. <u>John</u> threw <u>the pen</u> down.

____

b. <u>Mark and Keiran</u> climbed over <u>the sleeping children</u>.

____

Idioms. Explain 'to have an axe to grind' ______________

REVIEW

Term 1

1. Choose the word that fits.

imagine
numerous
conversation
carriage
procession
determine
senator
thoroughly
publication
defence

a. The decorated ___________ was drawn by two coal black horses.

b. They could not ___________ where the art treasures were hidden.

c. The ___________ was re-elected to parliament for a third term.

d. She stood below the stairs and overheard the ___________ between the two adults.

e. ___________ groups of children wandered in and out of the grounds.

f. The man was ___________ disgusted by the behaviour of the small group.

g. It was difficult to ___________ how the animal had been injured.

h. The ___________ was in circulation during the first week of the month.

2. Change these words to nouns.

a. vast ___________ c. subtract ___________ e. sincere ___________

b. similar ___________ d. correct ___________ f. music ___________

3. Change these words to adjectives.

a. haste ___________ c. youth ___________ e. competition ___________

b. secret ___________ d. science ___________ f. accept ___________

4. Underline and then rewrite incorrectly spelt words.

a. They did not corect there work well. ___________

b. The men will purchese the rifel here. ___________

c. She saw the intresting procesion. ___________

d. The burgler attracted the atention of the police. ___________

e. There was a serios problem with the rockit. ___________

f. The incedint took place near the councel yard. ___________

5. Rewrite the sentences correctly.

a. She will procede to the populer exercise center.

____

b. Do you remembre if a quartar of the diner was eatin?

____

c. The skillful worker was rewardded for his efort.

____

d. Did thay see the creture on the floting branch?

____

e. The soldier dived into the shalow water near the jettie.

____

6. Choose the correct word.

a. All of them walked ____________ the dense scrub. (threw, through)

b. They walked along the ____________ of the state. (border, boarder)

c. All of the children went there ____________ Shazia. (accept, except)

d. The Expedition travelled out into the ____________. (desert, dessert)

e. Did Alia come ____________ in her sprint event? (forth, fourth)

7. Write the plural form.

a. gas ____________ c. valley ____________ e. tomato ____________

b. injury ____________ d. knife ____________ f. success ____________

8. Build 5 words that are part of the word family for 'apply'.

____________ ____________ ____________ ____________ ____________

9. Use the prefix 'un', 'in', 'il' or 'ir' to build words.

a. not able to be resisted ____________

b. not or against the law ____________

c. not or the opposite of regular ____________

10. Write the three parts of these verbs.

a. surprise ____________ ____________ ____________

b. apply ____________ ____________ ____________

UNIT 9

probably	property
profit	prosperous
provide	protection
audience	attendance
sentence	endurance
ignorance	allowance
guidance	assistance

Extension

probability
properties
profitable
prosperity
provisional
protective
durable
ignorant
allowable
unassisted

____

____

1. WORD STUDY

There is a change in basic spelling to form some plurals.

e.g. louse — lice

Write the plural.

a. foot ___________ b. goose ___________

c. tooth ___________ d. woman ___________

e. ox ___________ f. mouse ___________

Some words don't change from singular to plural.

e.g. sheep, deer

List others.

g. ______________________________________

____

The prefix 'pro' means 'forth' or 'forward'.

e.g. prosper —
to go forward financially / good health

Match meanings and words.

h. to drive forward

i. to plan for the future

j. to speak clearly

k. to go forward

proceed
project
propel
pronounce

2. LOOKING AT verbs

Verbs can be <u>active</u> or <u>passive</u>.

e.g. She provided the new equipment. *(active)*

(The person or thing that is the subject of the sentence 'does' the action.)

The new equipment was provided by her. *(passive)*

(The doer of the action is not the subject of the sentence.)

Underline the verbs then write active or passive.

a. All the boys attended the meeting.

____

b. All the cartons were unloaded by the women. ___________

Rewrite in the passive form.

c. The woman saw the car.

____

d. Karen visited Elsa.

____

Rewrite in the active voice.

e. The car was washed by Kate.

____

3. word usage

Choose list and extension words.

a. The girl said that she would ___________ enter the swimming event.

b. The ___________ town grew wealthier after the discovery of gold.

c. The ___________ of the area from soil erosion was a difficult task.

d. The footballer showed he was very ___________ by not missing a game for eight seasons.

Elizabeth – Children's Friend PART 3

Sister Kenny believed it was necessary to treat the disease by relieving the contractions of the muscles.

She continued to treat children who came to her for assistance. Sadly there was no protection from the illness.

Elizabeth outlined her ideas at meetings, and gradually more medical people were in attendance in the audience. The guidance she provided was very important. Her methods began to be accepted throughout Australia and then overseas. Finally, in 1941, the United States National Foundation for Infantile Paralysis approved Sister Kenny's treatment of the disease.

A year later, after receiving many honours and opening clinics in several cities, she returned to Australia.

Sister Kenny died in 1942 at the age of sixty-six.

4. Select-A-WORD

Choose synonyms from the list.

a. flourishing __________ b. stamina __________

c. supply __________ d. support __________

e. direction __________

5. LOOKING AT nouns

Form nouns by adding the suffix 'ance' or 'ence' meaning 'state of being'.

a. annoy __________ b. resist __________

c. innocent __________ d. exist __________

e. absent __________

6. CORNER Challenge

Complete the CAT words.

a. a type of rocky waterfall
CAT________

b. underground tombs or burial places
CAT__________

c. a device for throwing stones or other projectiles
CAT________

d. a terrible event or disaster
CAT_____________

e. a list of items with prices or other details
CAT__________

f. a group or class of things
CAT________

g. something which is used in a chemical reaction
CAT________

7. Proof Reading

Rewrite the incorrect words correctly below.

articel carraige asent
soldier tongue intresting
libary numeros ocupation
exhibition serious similer

____

____

____

____

Famous people. What was named after Samuel Morse? ____________________

UNIT 10 Extension

advice	advertise
appeared	assembly
blood	boarder
humour	humorous
jealous	labour
harbour	honour
flavour	courage

advisable
advisory
advertiser
reappearance
humorously
jealousy
dishonourable
flavourings
courageous
encouraged

____

____

1. LOOKING AT adjectives

e.g. certain times, humorous events

Add adjectives.

a. __________ pearls

b. __________ work

c. __________ currents

List the adjectives in the last sentence of the text.

d. ____________________________

____

Adjectives can describe and compare things.

- **positive degree – telling about one thing**
  e.g. small
- **comparative degree – comparing two things**
  e.g. smaller
- **superlative degree – comparing more than two things**
  e.g. smallest

Write the degrees of comparison.

e. tiny __________ __________

f. fast __________ __________

g. lonely __________ __________

2. WORD STUDY

The suffix 'ous' means 'full of'.

e.g. humorous
— full of humour or fun

Use the ending 'ous' to build words.

a. __________ full of danger or peril

b. __________ full of grace

c. __________ full of anxiety

d. __________ full of wonder

e. __________ full of anger or fury

Add these beginnings to the items below.

ad	ap	as

f. ___vantage g. ___venture

h. ___peal i. ___sistant

j. ___parent k. ___sume

l. ___pliance m. ___plaud

Change these words to nouns by adding suitable suffixes.

n. advertise __________

o. appear __________

p. jealous __________

q. assemble __________

3. IDIOMS

An idiom is a common saying.

Explain these.

a. It breaks my heart to see her in such distress.

____

____

b. He did not have the information at his fingertips.

____

____

c. You should put your best foot forward with this project.

____

____

PART 1

Far North Experience

My name is Mebai Hawkin. I was born on the island of Mabuiag in 1920 and attended the local school. The rest of the world appeared very remote.

My first job was as a deckhand on a lugger working the reefs close to my home. We often had to labour from before sunrise to well past dark sorting the shells and cleaning the decks. The living conditions were very cramped on the boats.

Divers showed great courage, searching for pearls in the unknown reefs, wearing heavy suits and helmets. Frequently an injured diver had to be rushed to Thursday Island harbour for treatment. Sadly many died from the dreaded 'bends'. Despite the danger and hard work, many humorous events and funny experiences were had by all.

... continued on Page 24

4. word usage

Choose list words.

a. The kangaroo ____________ from behind the rocky ledge.

b. The ____________ story-teller amused the children.

c. The large trawler came into the ____________ yesterday.

d. The officer got a medal for her ____________ in the dangerous accident.

e. She will ____________ her car for sale in the local newspaper.

5. CORNER Challenge

Choose extension words.

a. All the different ____________ were added to the icecream vats.

b. The ____________ of the strange creature on three more nights puzzled everyone.

c. Although it was a ____________ effort the athlete did not win the race.

Explain what these words have in common.

e.g. 'tape' and 'disc' can both be used to record sounds and pictures.

d. | observation | telescope |

____

____

e. | punctual | chronometer |

____

____

6. Select-A-WORD

a. She gave them a lot of good ____________. (advice, advise)

b. The coach will ____________ them of the times for training. (advice, advise)

c. He had been a ____________ at the guest house for several months. (guest, guessed)

Idiom. Explain 'Her lips were sealed' ____________________

UNIT 11 Extension

belief	beginning
behaviour	brilliant
breathe	champion
chance	cheque
chamber	choir
character	flight
knelt	knowledge

believable
beginner
misbehaved
brilliance
breathless
championship
chanced
choral
chorus
flightless
____
____

1. LOOKING AT homophones

Homophones are words that sound alike but are spelt differently.

Choose the correct word.

stair	stare

a. That __________ needs to be mended.

b. Do not __________ at them.

waist	waste

c. He will __________ a lot of time.

d. She recorded her __________ measurement for the dressmaker.

plain	plane

e. They wandered out onto the __________.

f. The __________ was put into the hangar.

Write sentences using these pairs of words.

g. | lead | led |

____

____

h. | hire | higher |

____

____

2. WORD STUDY

The suffixes 'ship', 'hood' and 'ment' mean 'state of being'.

e.g. friendship
— state of being a friend

Add suffixes.

a. conceal______ b. owner______
c. measure______ d. priest______
e. improve______ f. child______

Write words to match the meanings.

g. ____________ment
state of being surprised

h. ____________hood
state of being a brother

i. __________ship
state of being an owner

Use these blends 'br', 'ch' or 'fl' with these endings.

j. ___igade k. ___imney
l. ___orus m. ___exible
n. ___ochure o. ___urry
p. ___uckle q. ___utter

3. Collective Nouns

Collective nouns are nouns that name a group of things, animals or people.

e.g. clump of trees

Name these groups.

a. __________ of actors
b. __________ of shady trees
c. __________ of piglets
d. __________ of singers
e. __________ of aircraft

Complete by adding the people, animals or things.

f. bunch of __________
g. fleet of __________
h. herd of __________
i. regiment of __________

PART 2

Far North Experience

In the early 1950s I was diving in a dangerous area, Darnley Deeps. At the beginning of my last season as a diver, I had the frightening belief that things would go wrong.

It was a fine day with a brilliant sky and calm conditions. I was thirty metres down on the ledge of a reef, when I stepped out and missed my footing. Simultaneously my air supply started to fade and I could hardly breathe. I began signalling frantically to those on the lugger as I rushed to the surface. Normally you come to the surface slowly, so I hoped someone would realise that I was in desperate trouble.

I passed out before I hit the deck. A flight was arranged to Cairns where I was placed in a decompression chamber to allow my body to recover. After that I was given a shore job at the pearling station where I have remained ever since, grateful to have lived through the diving mishap.

4. word usage

Use list and extension words.

a. All the vessels left the harbour at the ____________ of the day.

b. The ____________ she gained from studying science was great.

c. Although he was only a ____________ at the game, he was making progress.

d. The team competed in all the ____________ events.

e. People were amazed at the ____________ of the diamonds.

f. The emu and ostrich are ____________ birds.

5. CORNER Challenge

Choose extension words.

a. ____________ story

b. ____________ of the comet

c. ____________ birds

d. ____________ badly

Find words to fit the word frame.

e.

S					E
S					G

6. Select-A-WORD

Choose synonyms from the list.

a. dazzling ____________

b. commencement ____________

c. opportunity ____________

d. opinion ____________

7. Proof Reading

Rewrite with correct spelling and punctuation.

the briliant coir was begining to be regarded as chaimber music experts as they sang around the country. unfortunately there misbehavior on the flight was unbellievable

____

____

____

____

Proverbs. Explain 'All's well that ends well'. ____________

UNIT 12

airport	meanwhile
overhead	therefore
leisure	receipt
receive	seize
neighbour	dairy
jail	heaven
realise	theatre

Extension

aircraft
airstrip
airworthiness
overweight
overthrow
overhauling
oversupplied
seizure
neighbourhood
realisation

____

____

1. LOOKING AT *adjectival phrases*

An adjectival phrase describes the noun. A phrase begins with a preposition.

e.g. The tree with red flowers was planted.
noun *preposition*

Underline the adjectival phrases.

a. The pencils in the box belong to me.

b. The boxes with red lids are here.

c. The car with a green roof was going fast.

Add adjectival phrases.

d. The house ______________________________ has just been painted.

e. That ship ______________________________ sailed into the harbour early.

Use this adjectival phrase in a sentence.

f. near the stream

____

____

2. Direct Speech

Direct Speech shows the actual words a speaker uses. These words are enclosed between inverted commas. Begin the spoken words with a capital letter.

e.g. Jim laughingly declared, "She is a magician."
"We will search," said the tracker.

Add capitals, commas and quotation marks.

a. We begin our search today promised Karen.

b. The teacher said please use your ruler.

c. The librarian whispered look on the shelf dear

d. You pay half fare said the inspector.

3. WORD STUDY

The prefix 'over' means 'above'.

e.g. overhead — above the head

Write the words.

a. ____________ to look over or not notice

b. ____________ to flow over

c. ____________ to charge above the normal amount

d. ____________ to eat more than the usual

The prefix 'under' means 'beneath'.

e.g. underpay — pay less than the usual amount

Write the words.

e. ____________ to feed less than normal

f. ____________ beneath the usual weight

g. ____________ beneath the usual rules of the world

CARD DROP

The aim of the trick is to have your neighbour attempt to drop cards into a box. You, as Master of Card Drop, have no trouble completing the task, while they cannot manage to do so.

You will need a small box and a pack of cards.

- Select a person to attempt the task.
- Explain that they must drop the vertically held cards, from shoulder height, into the box.
- When they drop the cards, they will drop in an arc or series of arcs, and therefore miss the box.
- When it is your turn seize the card in a horizontal direction.

The demonstration will help everyone realise that when there is even pressure on the horizontal surface, the cards fall almost straight down.

5. CORNER Challenge

Choose extension words.

a. The workers were ___________ the machine.

b. The ___________ of the vessel by the patrol boat happened on Sunday.

c. Many new buildings have been erected in our ___________.

Explain the difference in meaning.

d. | inedible | indelible |

____

____

e. | bazaar | bizarre |

____

____

f. | personal | personnel |

____

____

4. word usage

Choose list words.

a. They did not ___________ that the ___________ was closed because of cyclonic weather.

b. A ___________ of ours went onto the stage to ___________ the award.

c. They will ___________ the heavy rope to tie up the barge.

d. During her ___________ time she studied painting.

e. Was the ___________ given to the customer?

6. Select-A-WORD

a. The boy wrote in his ___________ every evening. (diary, dairy)

b. Has he ___________ the present? (receipt, received)

Use a thesaurus to find synonyms.

c. grasp ___________

d. acquire ___________

e. understand ___________

f. recreation ___________

Proverbs. Explain 'Better half a loaf than no bread'. ___________

UNIT 13 Extension

parcel	palace
pastime	pastures
parallel	particular
occupy	occurred
occasionally	planet
plaster	plastic
platform	pleasure

parcelled
palatial
pasteurise
pasteurisation
parallelogram
occupant
occupation
occurrence
planetary
displeasure
____
____

1. LOOKING AT adverbs

Adverbs tell us more about the meaning of verbs, adjectives or other adverbs. They describe *how*, *when* and *where* and often end in 'ly'.

e.g. He was really sorry.
She left early.
Can I go there?

Underline the adverb and circle the word it describes.

e.g. John (listened) carefully.

a. Several of the birds flew slowly across the treetops.

b. That flight will be leaving soon.

c. She said she was very tired.

Add adverbs.

d. Many of them walked __________ in the park __________.

e. The food was found __________ and __________ beside the creek.

Add the suffix 'ly' to these words.

f. heaven___ g. great___ h. contented___

2. WORD STUDY

These words derive from Greek.
The prefix 'para' means 'beside'.

Match the words and meanings.

paragraph parallel
parasite parable

a. something running or placed exactly beside another __________
b. a distinct portion of writing dealing with a point __________
c. a tale that has a meaning beside the story itself __________
d. something which lives beside, on or in a host __________

The suffix 'ise' means 'to make'.

e.g. 'pasteurise' means 'to make pure or germ free'.

Complete.

e. to make civil __________
f. to make comments against something __________
g. to make fertile __________

Add prefixes and suffixes to 'occupy'.

h. ____________________
____

3. LOOKING AT gender

Nouns and pronouns can be masculine, feminine, common or neuter.

e.g. cow *(feminine)* — bull *(masculine)*
calf *(common: male or female)*
rock *(neuter: neither male or female)*

Write the opposites.

a. mother __________
b. colt __________
c. fox __________
d. gander __________

Write the letters M, F, C or N

e. children ( ) f. lioness ( )
g. bread ( ) h. animal ( )
i. water ( ) j. count ( )

PART 1

Bird Migration

Bird migration is one particular puzzle that has interested scientists for centuries. Although we have a good general idea of the paths taken, much is still to be discovered. There are over eight thousand species of birds, many of which are migratory. Their twice yearly journeys cross whole continents and oceans all over the planet.

The Arctic Tern travels further than other migratory birds. After a short breeding season, it heads south. Passing the warmer pastures of the temperate lands, it crosses the Atlantic Ocean to Europe and down the coast of Africa to the edge of Antarctica.

Migrations have occurred for thousands of years and the study of the actual paths will occupy scientific investigation for many years. Occasionally amateur bird watchers help with sightings and bird banding.

... continued on Page 30

5. CORNER Challenge

Choose extension words.

a. The __________ of the milk took place in that factory.

b. The villagers were puzzled by the strange __________.

c. The untidy work caused the employer a great deal of __________.

Buildings

e.g. A granary is where grain is stored.

d. An __________ is where rubbish is burned.

e. A __________ is where medicine is stored.

f. A __________ is where stone is mined.

4. word usage

Add suffixes.

a. The workers were parcel_____ up the bundles of leaflets.

b. The children were particular_____ pleased with the presents.

c. The family has occup_____ this piece of land for years.

d. All of these events will be occur_____ during the afternoon.

e. After the wall had been plaster_____, it was sanded.

6. Proverbs

Proverbs are common sayings illustrating a belief or truth.

Explain them.

a. First come first served.

____

____

b. Charity begins at home.

____

____

c. He who hesitates is lost.

____

____

Proverbs. Explain 'Every dog has its day' ______________________________

UNIT 14

machinery	magnificent
marvellous	married
masculine	mathematics
maximum	majority
mayor	media
meteor	minimum
minister	mysterious

Extension

mechanise
mechanical
mechanisation
magnificence
mathematical
minority
meteorite
administer
administrative
mysteriously
____
____

1. LOOKING AT *language*

The Latin root 'finis' means 'the end'.

finale	define	superfine	final
finish	refine	unfinished	confine

Choose the correct word.

a. The __________ event on the sports program was the 800 metre race.

b. After the __________ of the concert people left the arena.

c. The machine was designed to __________ the substance into its purest form.

d. The warders will __________ the prisoners to their barracks.

The Latin word 'clamo' means 'to shout'.

Match the words to meanings.

e. to announce publicly
f. to cry out loudly
g. lots of noise or shouting
h. the act of giving or shouting out news publicly

clamour
proclaim
proclamation
exclaim

2. WORD STUDY

Write the plural.

a. mystery __________
b. minister __________
c. viola __________
d. mouse __________
e. thief __________
f. speech __________
g. brother-in-law __________
h. cupful __________
i. radius __________
j. oasis __________

3. Direct Speech

Add quotation marks, capitals and commas.

a. I wrote the book several years ago said the author

b. The captain ordered find out the truth

c. Move along ordered the bus inspector

d. The announcer called next stop Newtown

If the spoken words are interrupted by 'she said' a comma is used before and after 'she said'.

e.g. "I have athletics training," said Jim, "this afternoon."

Punctuate.

e. My teacher needs my help said Mary and then I will go home

f. Where is the closest beach asked Pip I want to go there today

Bird Migration

Bird banding, which is the fastening of numbered bands around the legs of birds without the use of special machinery, helps us track bird movement around the world. Birds are captured, banded and then set free. Anyone finding a bird sends the number to one of the stations. The movement of the birds can then be worked out.

The majority of migratory birds breed in the Northern Hemisphere, where there is larger land area allowing them maximum room for nesting and obtaining food.

The swallow, a marvellous example, spends its winters in the Southern Hemisphere. It flies only by day, feeding as it flies across the Mediterranean, round the Sahara Desert to Central Africa. On its return it flies directly over the Sahara, reducing its distance to a minimum.

5. CORNER Challenge

Explain the different meaning of the words.

a. | vocation | vacation |

____

____

____

b. | confirm | conform |

____

____

____

c. | access | excess |

____

____

____

d. | industrial | industrious |

____

____

____

4. Select-A-WORD

Choose antonyms of the list words to complete.

a. The __________ sight of the atomic explosion was never forgotten by the few survivors.

b. All of the __________ people working on the project were housed in the large dormitories.

c. The absolute __________ number of people to view the temple was set at five persons.

d. In the community a __________ of people favoured the construction of the dam.

6. Vocabulary

Circle the more suitable word.

a. The manager said that the buyer/customer was perfectly correct.

b. After the concert the people enjoyed light foods/refreshments.

c. The woman owned some very dear/expensive jewellery.

Write a sentence showing the meaning of this pair of words

d. | serious | solemn | ______________________

____

____

Proverbs. Explain 'Curiosity killed the cat' ______________________

UNIT 15 Extension

persist	perimeter
persuade	personal
percentage	permanent
principal	principle
quality	quantity
quarrel	excellent
experience	executive

persistence
periscope
persuasion
personality
impersonal
permanence
qualify
qualifications
quarrelsome
excellence
____
____

1. LOOKING AT *relative pronouns*

Joining words stand as close as possible to nouns or pronouns to which they refer.

- **who – used for people**
  e.g. The man who . . .
- **that – used with people / things / animals**
  e.g. The shoe that I . . .
- **which – used with animals / things**
  e.g. The dog which . . .
- **whom – used after a preposition**
  e.g. The boy of whom . . .

Underline the noun to which the relative pronoun refers.

a. Return this book to the girl whose parents are here.

b. He has a car that is made of plastic.

c. A snake that is poisonous is not a suitable pet.

Add 'which', 'that', 'whose', 'who' or 'whom'.

d. Did you speak to the man ________ brother travelled to Mexico?

e. This is the woman ________ went to China.

f. These are the people from ________ we bought the used car.

2. LOOKING AT *language*

Use a dictionary to find the meanings and country of origin of these words.

a. springbok ____________
____
country of origin: ________

b. gaucho ____________
____
country of origin: ________

c. rajah ____________
____
country of origin: ________

d. tycoon ____________
____
country of origin: ________

e. chef ____________
____
country of origin: ________

3. WORD STUDY

The Greek prefix 'peri' means 'round' or 'around'.

Explain the meanings using 'round' or 'about' in your answer.

a. perimeter ____________
____

b. periscope ____________
____

Form adjectives using the suffixes.

al	ent	ive	some

c. persist____ d. quarrel____

e. person____ f. persuade____

Use prefixes 'im' or 'in'.

g. ____personal h. ____possible

i. ____permanent j. ____attentive

Write four words with the root 'meter'.

k. ________ ________
________ ________

4 Alandale Road,
Southend.
14 July, 1998.

Hi, Giselle,

Just a note to let you know about last weekend.

Peta and I went on an excellent rock climb. We set out in the land rover at seven o'clock in the morning. We travelled to Malins Peak where there is a permanent camp on the top slopes. The beginner's rock climb began down in the wide valley and went up to the cliffs on the other side. We carried a huge quantity of ropes and gear with us.

First we had to practise with ropes and cables. We had to persist until we felt comfortable using them. Then we could begin the real climb. Peta and I managed three successful climbs. It was an experience that I won't forget.

See you next weekend.

Tegan

6. CORNER Challenge

Complete the crossword puzzle.

a. a group of soldiers
b. to accept
c. synonym for bravery
d. an opportunity
e. a group of words
f. a group of people organising something
g. material or element
h. to fight or argue
i. not a copy
j. 'shooting star'

4. word usage

Add an adjective and list word.

a. A __________ __________ of the people in the city attended the concert.
b. The __________ __________ goods were bought in large numbers by people.
c. A __________ __________ broke out between the families.

5. Vocabulary

Words to describe small quantities.

e.g. speck of dust

a. a sip of ____________________
b. a grain of ____________________
c. a morsel of ____________________
d. a sliver of ____________________

7. Select-A-WORD

a. The __________ of the school presented the awards. (principle, principal)
b. The __________ cause of the accident was excessive speed. (principle, principal)
c. A large __________ of the material was removed. (quantity, quality)
d. The suit was of excellent __________. (quantity, quality)

Idiom. Explain 'To break the ice' ________________________________

UNIT 16 Extension

colony	culture
agriculture	manuscript
manual	manufacture
populate	population
publisher	republic
instruct	obstruct
construct	structure

colonise
colonial
agricultural
scribe
depopulated
popularity
republican
reconstruction
obstruction
structural

____

____

1. LOOKING AT punctuation

Commas separate nouns and adjectives in a list.
e.g. Jason, Kao and Lana went to Sydney.
Commas mark off words or phrases that give a noun or pronoun another name.
e.g. The girl, Tanya, is my sister.
Corfu, one of the Greek islands, is a resort.
Commas are used for introductory statements.
e.g. When the storm passed, we could see the damage.

Insert commas.

a. Her cat Leila was on the verandah.
b. Shun Maria Valerio Kim and Tegan have been to the theatre.
c. There were indeed several people there.
d. Lillie one of Australia's greatest bowlers retired in 1984.
e. Arriving at the house he realised he was too late.

Proof reading.

f. the publisher restructtured the agriculturel manuel which instructed the farmers.

____

____

2. WORD STUDY

These list words have Latin roots.

'manus' – hand
e.g. manufacture — make by hand

manage manual manacle

'colo' – to till or cultivate

cultivation colonise cultivate

'populus' – the people

populate populous unpopular

Choose words to fit.

a. She could not ____________ to complete the work on time.
b. The ____________ was placed on the prisoner when he returned.
c. The ____________ of the crop brought prosperity to the district.
d. The decision he made was an ____________ one.

3. word usage

Use verbs formed from list words.

a. The farmers in this district have been ____________ the fertile lands since 1900.
b. Many of those products were ____________ in Victoria.
c. The road was ____________ by the accident.
d. All the workers were ____________ in the safety procedures at the factory.
e. "Has that book been ____________ yet?" she asked.
f. That part of the country was ____________ many years ago.

The Industrial Area

Where once agriculture was the main use of this land, there is now an immense industrial area and the population has risen.

Stretching for almost a kilometre along the eastern boundary are numerous structures housing huge machines which manufacture motor vehicle parts and steel sheds. A maze of bitumen roads, some with temporary road blocks to obstruct the progress of delivery trucks, link these gigantic buildings. Manual labourers construct buildings and earthmoving equipment has changed the look of the landscape for ever.

The thud and clang of the heavy machinery resonates through the valleys. Easterly winds blow clouds of dust across the area, leaving layers of dust particles on everything.

5. CORNER Challenge

Complete the ANT words.

a. being plentiful
________ANT

b. being conceited
________ANT

c. not knowing anything
________ANT

d. very large or huge
_____ANT___

e. happening all the time
________ANT

f. being courageous
_______ANT

4. Joining

Sentences can begin with past participles when joined.

e.g. He was thrown by the horse.
He fell heavily to the ground.
Thrown by the horse, he fell heavily to the ground.

a. The army was defeated by the enemy.
The army retreated.

____

____

b. Jack was knocked over by the force.
Jack sat down to recover.

____

____

c. The tree was blown by the wind.
The tree fell over.

____

____

6. Using Extension Words

a. The ____________ machinery was stored in the farmer's sheds.

b. The inventors were delighted by the ____________ of the new computer game.

c. The ____________ on the road held up the traffic.

d. The settlers decided to ____________ the isolated area.

7. Abstract Nouns

Form an abstract noun from the underlined words.

a. A thief is arrested for __________.

b. A slave has to suffer a life of __________.

c. A sadistic person is known for their __________.

d. A tyrant is known for their __________.

Idiom. Explain 'To throw cold water on (something)' ______________________________

REVIEW Term 2

1. Choose the word that fits.

manuscript
endurance
permanent
behaviour
realise
masculine
harbour
seize
occasionally

a. The ___________ race was difficult for horse and rider.
b. The new cruiser steamed into the ___________.
c. Father said that good ___________ would be rewarded.
d. It was difficult for the man in the water to ___________ the rope.
e. Did you ___________ that our team has won ten games?
f. Only ___________ were boarders allowed to go on unescorted trips.
g. Animals will die if there is no ___________ supply of water.
h. The author completed the ___________ within fourteen days.

2. Change these verbs to adjectives.

a. ignore ___________ b. persuade___________ c. honour ___________
d. excel ___________ e. help ___________ f. colonise ___________

3. Change these words to nouns.

a. provide ___________ b. realise ___________ c. magnificent ___________
d. instruct ___________ e. appear ___________ f. populate ___________

4. Underline incorrectly spelt words. Rewrite correctly.

a. At the begining of the fortnite they started work. ___________
b. The people in the coleny had to work evry day. ___________
c. The machinary was placed in paralel rows. ___________
d. Many of the manuel workers toiled on the harbour foreshore ___________
e. The marvelous display gave the on-lookers a grate deal of pleasere. ___________

5. Rewrite the sentences correctly.

a. The peple past this way on there way to the waterfal.

____

b. We whent by oreself to the orchard on the oposite side of the rode.

____

c. She brought thoes diferent chairs at that adress.

____

d. All injoyed a deliteful diner on the verinda.

____

e. We are going to prepear for the importent examinition.

____

6. Choose the correct word.

a. Will you tie up the ___________ with the other ponies please? (mayor, mare)

b. The ___________ of the school welcomed the visitors. (principal, principle)

c. Anna was short of ___________ after the long distance run. (breath, breathe)

d. The ___________ at the factory met to discuss their future. (personal, personnel)

7. Correct the underlined words if they are incorrectly spelt.

a. It was a <u>weird</u> looking costume. ___________

b. They did not <u>recieve</u> the present early. ___________

c. Did they give you a <u>receipt</u> for the money? ___________

8. Build six words that are part of the word family for 'real'.

__________ __________ __________ __________ __________ __________

9. Write in the plural form.

a. minister ___________ c. mouse ___________ e. oasis ___________

b. theory ___________ d. radio ___________ f. mother-in-law ___________

10. Use correctly in sentences.

a. unpopular ____

b. cultivation ____

UNIT 17 Extension

announcer	customer
calculator	employer
messenger	traveller
assistant	attendance
inhabitant	spectator
governor	survivor
emperor	governess

announcement
customise
unemployable
employee
assistance
unattended
habitable
spectacle
survival
empress
____
____

1. LOOKING AT adjectival phrases & prepositions

e.g. The chart (on) the shelf is mine.

Underline the adjectival phrases and circle the prepositions.

a. The car with a red roof belongs to Sue.

b. The hills in the distance are thickly forested.

c. The girl in the red tracksuit is a fine athlete.

Add adjectival phrases.

d. I saw the boy ____________________.

e. That old house ____________________ is in need of repair.

Use in sentences.

f. with a blue shirt ____________________

g. of great size ____________________

2. PUNCTUATION

Add capital letters and quotation marks.

a. Well asked the boy when are you going to collect it?

b. Are you going to visit your aunt robyn in bega asked paul.

2. ABBREVIATIONS

This is the shortened form of a word.

- **When the first and last letters of a word are used no full stop is used.**
  e.g. advt
- **When the first few letters are used then a full stop is used.**
  e.g. exam.
- **Full stops are used between single letters standing for words.**
  e.g. P.M. (Prime Minister)

Write what these abbreviations stand for.

a. R.S.L. ____________

b. N.R.M.A. ____________

c. Dr ____________

d. Rev. ____________

e. J.P. ____________

f. Prof. ____________

g. anon. ____________

h. temp. ____________

i. soc. ____________

j. Mr ____________

4. CONJUNCTIONS

Join sentences using these words.

until where unless how because

a. We knew he was hurt ________ we saw the accident.

b. I can't go ________ I do my homework.

c. He will have to wait ________ the bus arrives.

d. Jeremy left the biscuits ________ we could find them.

e. The keeper explained ________ radar is used by bats.

ANSWERS

UNIT 1
Page 1-2

1. **NOUNS**
   a. Gold, Victoria, haste, settlers, fortunes
   b. boy, ankle, panic
   c. rush, problems
   d. Amanda, Tegan, Leah, Jenolan, Caves, Thursday
   e. Mr Truscott, Wagga Wagga
2. **WORD STUDY**
   a. ditches
   b. climaxes
   c. brushes
   d. mattresses
   e. buzzes
   f. accept
   g. ascent
   h. panic
   i. vast
   j. reapply, applies, applied, applying
3. **SELECT-A-WORD**
   a. except
   b. accept
   c. ascend
   d. ascent
   e. engine
4. **WORD USAGE**
   a. accept b. apply
   c. carriage d. vast
   e. harvest f. haste
5. **CHALLENGE CORNER**
   a. application
   b. applicant
   c. vastness
   d. Answers will vary.
6. **PROOF READING**
   a. ascent, mountain
   b. articles, carriage

ANAGRAM
Canter

UNIT 2
Page 3-4

1. **NOUNS**
   a. astonishment, dismay
   b. sadness, despair
   c. friendship d. wisdom
   e. honesty f. magician
   g. musician
2. **WORD STUDY**
   a. cities b. territories
   c. injuries d. comedies
   e. imagines, imagined, imagining, imaginative, imagination, imaginary, unimagined
   f. imaginative
   g. imagination h. imaginary
3. **DICTIONARY WORK**
   a. imbalance b. incident
   c. Chiraasi, Elise, Hayna, Howard, Jennet, Nadiya, Shazia, Sherin, Shunling, Tai, Tonya
4. **STATEMENTS & QUESTIONS**
   Verbs will vary.
   a. Statement b. Statement
   c. Question
5. **CHALLENGE CORNER**
   a. galaxy/constellation
   b. vineyard c. suite
   d. anthology e. batch
   f. congregation g. necessity
   h. anxiety i. savagery
   j. remainder k. suggestion
6. **SELECT-A-WORD**
   a. figure b. immediate
   c. imaginary d. liquid
   e. interesting f. fiction
   g. tight h. fiction

SAYINGS
To pretend to be upset. Originates from the belief that a crocodile shed tears while devouring its victim.

UNIT 3
Page 5-6

1. **VERBS**
   a. found, to co-operate, was held
   b-f. Answers will vary.
2. **WORD STUDY**
   a. chimneys b. storeys
   c. quays d. volleys
   e. correct f. mobile
   g. bore h. borrow
   i. irregular j. insincere
   k. illegal l. illegible
3. **EXTENSION WORDS**
   a. borrower
   b. mobilization
   c. co-operatively
   d. forthwith
   e. mobility
   f. mobilize, mobility, mobilization, mobilizable, mobiliser
4. **WORD USAGE**
   a. boring
   b. borrowed
   c. bordering
   d. worshipped
   e. co-operation
5. **CHALLENGE CORNER**
   a. Answers will vary.
   b. active
   c. objective
   d. progressive
   e. ceaseless
   f. boarder
   g. boarder
6. **PROOF READING**
   border, soldier, fourth, borrowed, towel

ANAGRAM
merit

UNIT 4
Page 7-8

1. **VERBS**
   a. cover, depends, are made up, consist
   b. future
   c. past
   d. present
   e. is selecting, has selected
   f. is throwing, has thrown
2. **WORD STUDY**
   a. halves b. wharves
   c. thieves d. yourselves
   e. miserable f. audible
   g. edible h. visible
3. **WORD USAGE**
   Adjectives will vary.
   a. section b. service
   c. senator d. secretary
4. **SELECT-A-WORD**
   a. secret b. serious
   c. silence d. signature
   e. simplify
5. **CHALLENGE CORNER**
   a. worship b. incident
   c. bitumen d. co-operate
   e. applying f. liquid
   g. ascent h. section
   i. hastily j. drying
6. **EXTENSION WORDS**
   a. seriously
   b. serviceable
   c. silently
   d. secretive

CLOTHING
a. Fez – A Turkish cap that is a tasselled, red, truncated cone.
b. Busby – A tall fur hat which has a bag hanging off the right side. Worn by the Hussars in the British Army.

ANSWERS

UNIT 5
Page 9-10

1. **PRONOUNS**
   a. she, her, their
   b. you, it
   c. My, us, we, their
   d. you, me
   e. Our, us, they
   f-g. Answers will vary.
2. **WORD STUDY**
   a. buffaloes b. potatoes
   c. volcanoes d. tomatoes
   e. rodeos f. solos
   g. trios h. radios
   i. manager j. shopper
   k. porter l. fruiterer
3. **SELECT-A-WORD**
   a. usable
   b. useful
   c. useless
   d. usefully
4. **WORD USAGE**
   a. public
   b. purchase
   c. unique
   d. numerous
   e-h. Answers will vary.
5. **CHALLENGE CORNER**
   a. Answers will vary.
   b. Aristocrat
   c. autocrat
   d. democrat
   e-g. Answers will vary.
6. **EXTENSION WORDS**
   a. publication
   b. musical
   c. budgeting
   d. reusable
   e. Answers will vary.

OCCUPATIONS
A man employed to load and unload ships.

UNIT 6
Page 11-12

1. **LANGUAGE**
   a. depot b. impostor
   c. compose d. preposition
   e. opponent f. dispose
   g. Answers will vary
2. **WORD STUDY**
   a. contribution b. attraction
   c. weariness d. brightness
   e. happiness f. caution
   g. permission h. heroes
   i. successes j. stretches
   k. youthful
   l. ruinous
   m.guilty
3. **VOCABULARY**
   a. dispute b. depart
   c. opportunity d. interior
   e. grateful
4. **WORD USAGE**
   Verbs will vary.
   a. council b. tourists
   c. guide d. suitable
   e. youth
5. **CHALLENGE CORNER**
   a. production b. conductor
   c. education d. reduction
   e. conductor f. education
   g. production h. reduction
6. **SELECT-A-WORD**
   a. thought
   b. Though
   c. thorough

FAMOUS PEOPLE
a. the watt, a unit of energy
b. pasteurisation, the sterilization of milk

UNIT 7
Page 13-14

1. **LANGUAGE**
   a emit b. dismiss
   c. transmit d. missile
   e. corridor f. cursory
2. **WORD STUDY**
   a. submerge b. submit
   c. submarine d. suppress
   e. suspend f. subtract
   g. suffer h. successive
   i. substantial
   j. defendable / defensive
   k. desirable
3. **VOCABULARY**
   a. a room or few rooms in a building occupied by others
   b. light outdoor structure for the sale of food, newspapers, etc.
   c. the part of the building occupied by the audience.
   d. a large tent
   e. a cottage at the gates of the grounds of a large house
4. **WORD USAGE**
   a. substantial
   b. unscientific
   c. determination
   d. subtraction
5. **CHALLENGE CORNER**
   a. prospector b. spectacle
   c. spectators d. suspect
   e. spectacle f. spectators
   g. suspect h. prospector
6. **PROOF READING**
   The scientist was determined to collect sufficient scientific data so that he could definitely defend his theses.

OCCUPATION
A person who collects stamps.

UNIT 8
Page 15-16

1. **PUNCTUATION**
   a. Has your brother Craig read the book 'The Sheltered Cove' by Alan Rawson?
   b. Meg, Tejan and Cheryn went to Maitland last July.
   c. Does Jessica Hsieh live in Canyan Road, Harrisville?
   d. The countries of Great Britain are England, Wales, Scotland and Ireland.
   e. "Have the Laird Brothers ever been to Bega on the southern coast of New South Wales?" asked Ellen.
   f. "I do not know exactly where it has gone," the boy said clearly.
2. **WORD STUDY**
   a. extension b. contribution
   c. occasion d. affection
   e. caution f. to attend
   g. to proceed h. to operate
   i. to exhibit
3. **EXTENSION WORDS**
   a. affectionately
   b. introductory
   c. occupier
   d. opposing
4. **WORD USAGE**
   a. competed
   b. introduced
   c. permitted
   d. proceed
5. **CHALLENGE CORNER**
   Answers will vary.
6. **PRONOUNS**
   a. He threw it down.
   b. They climbed over them.

IDIOMS
To have something to complain about

ANSWERS

UNIT 9
Page 19-20

1. **WORD STUDY**
   a. feet b. geese
   c. teeth d. women
   e. oxen f. mice
   g. e.g. fish, scissors, tweezers salmon, jeans
   h. propel i. project
   j. pronounce k. proceed
2. **VERBS**
   a. attended active
   b. unloaded passive
   c. The car was seen by the woman.
   d. Elsa was visited by Karen.
   e. Kate washed the car.
3. **WORD USAGE**
   a. probably b. prosperous
   c. protection d. durable
4. **SELECT-A-WORD**
   a. prosperous b. endurance
   c. provide d. assistance
   e. guidance
5. **NOUNS**
   a. annoyance
   b. resistance
   c. innocence
   d. existence
   e. absence
6. **CHALLENGE CORNER**
   a. cataract b. catacombs
   c. catapult d. catastrophe
   e. catalogue f. category
   g. catalyst
7. **PROOF READING**
   article, carriage, ascent, interesting, library, numerous, occupation, similar

FAMOUS PEOPLE
Morse Code

UNIT 10
Page 21-22

1. **ADJECTIVES**
   a-c. Answers will vary.
   d. hard, humorous, funny
   e. tinier, tiniest
   f. faster, fastest
   g. lonelier, loneliest
2. **WORD STUDY**
   a. dangerous/perilous
   b. gracious c. anxious
   d. wondrous e. furious
   f. advantage g. adventure
   h. appeal i. assistant
   j. apparent k. assume
   l. appliance m. applaud
   n. advertising/advertisement
   o. appearance/appearing
   p. jealousy q. assembly
3. **IDIOMS**
   a. It makes me very upset.
   b. Readily available
   c. Work hard and try to do your best work
4. **WORD USAGE**
   a. appeared
   b. humorous
   c. harbour
   d. courage
   e. advertise
5. **CHALLENGE CORNER**
   a. flavourings b. reappearance
   c. courageous
   d. both relate to watching something closely
   e. both have to do with accurate time keeping
6. **SELECT-A-WORD**
   a. advice b. advise
   c. guest

IDIOM
She wouldn't tell anyone the secret.

UNIT 11
Page 23-24

1. **HOMOPHONES**
   a. stair b. stare c. waste
   d. waist e. plain f. plane
   g-h. Answers will vary.
2. **WORD STUDY**
   a. concealment
   b. ownership
   c. measurement
   d. priesthood
   e. improvement
   f. childhood
   g. astonishment
   h. brotherhood
   i. ownership
   j. brigade k. chimney
   l. chorus m. flexible
   n. brochure o. flurry
   p. chuckle q. flutter
3. **COLLECTIVE NOUNS**
   a. troupe b. avenue
   c. litter d. choir
   e. squadron f. flowers
   g. ships h. cattle
   i. soldiers
4. **WORD USAGE**
   a. beginning b. knowledge
   c. beginner d. championship
   e. brilliance f. flightless
5. **CHALLENGE CORNER**
   a. believable b. brilliance
   c. flightless d. misbehaved
   e. Answers will vary.
6. **SELECT-A-WORD**
   a. brilliant b. beginning
   c. chance d. belief
7. **PROOF READING**
   The brilliant choir, beginning, chamber, Unfortunately, their misbehaviour, unbelievable

PROVERBS
If everything works out well, all problems are solved.

UNIT 12
Page 25-26

1. **ADJECTIVAL PHRASES**
   a. in the box
   b. with red lids
   c. with a green roof
   d-f. Answers will vary.
2. **DIRECT SPEECH**
   a. "We begin our search today," promised Karen.
   b. The teacher said, "Please use your ruler."
   c. The librarian whispered, "Look on the shelf dear."
   d. "You pay half fare," said the inspector.
3. **WORD STUDY**
   a. overlook b. overflow
   c. overcharge d. overeat
   e. underfeed f. underweight
   g. underworld
4. **WORD USAGE**
   a. realise, airport
   b. neighbour, receive
   c. seize
   d. leisure
   e. receipt
5. **CHALLENGE CORNER**
   a. overhauling
   b. seizure
   c. neighbourhood
   d. unable to be eaten; ink that can not be removed
   e. an oriental market; strange happening
   f. one's own, individual; people working in an office
6. **SELECT-A-WORD**
   a. diary
   b. received
   c-f. Answers may vary.

PROVERBS
Be content with what have, don't always want more.

ANSWERS

UNIT 13
Page 27-28

1. **ADVERBS**
   a. V-flew; Ad-slowly
   b. V-will be leaving; Ad-soon
   c. Adj-tired, Ad-very
   d-e. Answers will vary.
   f. heavenly g. greatly
   h. contentedly
2. **WORD STUDY**
   a. parallel b. paragraph
   c. parable d. parasite
   e. civilise f. criticise
   g. fertilise
   h. occupies, occupied, unoccupied, occupying
3. **GENDER**
   a. father b. filly
   c. vixen d. goose
   e. C f. F g. N
   h. C i. N j. M
4. **WORD USAGE**
   a. parcelling b. particularly
   c. occupied d. occurring
   e. plastered
5. **CHALLENGE CORNER**
   a. pasteurisation
   b. occurrence
   c. displeasure d. incinerator
   e. pharmacy f. quarry
6. **PROVERBS**
   a. If you arrive first you will have the pick.
   b. Show by your example.
   c. Don't wait to start if you're ready, you may lose your chance.

PROVERBS
Everyone will eventually have a chance to shine.

UNIT 14
Page 29-30

1. **LANGUAGE**
   a. final b. finale
   c. refine d. confine
   e. proclaim f. exclaim
   g. clamour h. proclamation
2. **WORD STUDY**
   a. mysteries b. ministers
   c. violas d. mice
   e. thieves f. speeches
   g. brothers-in-law
   h. cupfuls i. radii j. oases
3. **DIRECT SPEECH**
   a. "I wrote the book several years ago," said the author.
   b. The captain ordered, "Find out the truth."
   c. "Move along," ordered the bus inspector.
   d. The announcer called, "Next stop Newtown."
   e. "My teacher needs my help," said Mary, "and then I will go home."
   f. "Where is the closest beach?" asked Pip, "I want to go there today."
4. **SELECT-A-WORD**
   a. terrifying b. single
   c. maximum/minimum
   d. majority/minority
5. **CHALLENGE CORNER**
   a. divine call to a career; a holiday
   b. establish more firmly; form according to a pattern
   c. right or means to approach; overstepping the limit
   d. of industries; diligent, hard working
6. **VOCABULARY**
   a. customer
   b. refreshments
   c. expensive
   d. Answers will vary

PROVERB
Inquisitiveness can ruin what is planned to happen.

UNIT 15
Page 31-32

1. **RELATIVE PRONOUNS**
   a. girl b. car c. snake
   d. whose e. who f. whom
2. **LANGUAGE**
   a. a gazelle – South Africa
   b. a native cowboy of mixed Indian and Spanish descent – South America
   c. a king or prince – India
   d. a businessman having great wealth and power – Japan/China
   e. a head cook – France
3. **WORD STUDY**
   a. The outer boundary of a two-dimensional shape
   b. an optical instrument used to view the surface of water when standing below or behind
   c. persistent d. quarrelsome
   e. personal f. persuasive
   g. impersonal h. impossible
   i. impermanent j. inattentive
   k. Answers will vary
4. **WORD USAGE**
   Adjectives will vary.
   a. percentage b. quality
   c. quarrel
5. **VOCABULARY**
   a. water b. sand
   c. food d. wood
6. **CHALLENGE CORNER**
   a. company b. receive
   c. courage d. chance
   e. sentence f. council
   g. substance h. quarrel
   i. original j. meteor
7. **SELECT-A-WORD**
   a. principal b. principle
   c. quantity d. quality

IDIOM to prepare the way (e.g. for conversation)

UNIT 16
Page 33-34

1. **PUNCTUATION**
   a. Her cat, Leila,
   b. Shun, Maria, Valerio, Kim and Tegan
   c. There were, indeed,
   d. Lillie, one of Australia's greatest bowlers,
   e. Arriving at the house, he
   f. The publisher restructured the agricultural manual which instructed the farmers.
2. **WORD STUDY**
   a. manage b. manacle
   c. cultivation d. unpopular
3. **WORD USAGE**
   a. cultivating
   b. manufactured
   c. obstructed
   d. instructed
   e. published
   f. populated
4. **SENTENCES**
   a. Defeated by the enemy, the army retreated.
   b. Knocked over by the force, Jack sat down to recover.
   c. Blown by the wind, the tree fell over.
5. **CHALLENGE CORNER**
   a. abundant b. arrogant
   c. ignorant d. gigantic
   e. constant f. valiant
6. **EXTENSION WORDS**
   a. agricultural b. popularity
   c. obstruction d. colonise
7. **ABSTRACT NOUNS**
   a. theft b. slavery
   c. sadism d. tyranny

IDIOM
to discourage

ANSWERS

UNIT 17
Page 37-38

1. **ADJECTIVAL PHRASES**
   a. with a red roof
   b. in the distance
   c. in the red tracksuit
   d-g. Answers will vary.
2. **PUNCTUATION**
   a. "Well," asked the boy, "when are you going to collect it?"
   b. "Are you going to visit your Aunt Robyn in Bega?" asked Paul.
3. **ABBREVIATIONS**
   a. Returned Services League.
   b. National Roads and Motorists Association
   c. Doctor d. Reverend
   e. Justice of the Peace
   f. Professor g. anonymous
   h. temperature i. society
   j. Mister
4. **CONJUNCTIONS**
   a. because b. unless
   c. until d. where e. how
5. **SELECT-A-WORD**
   a. survivor b. messenger
   c. spectator d. customer
   e. inhabitant f. employer
   g. traveller h. busker
   i. blacksmith / farrier j. curator
6. **CHALLENGE CORNER**
   a. spectacle b. anouncement
   c. unattended d. habitable
   e. empress
   f. Answers will vary.
7. **DICTIONARY WORK**
   a. fossick b. intense
   c. mortify d. prepare
   e. schedule f. dwindle
   g. habitable

ANALOGIES empress

UNIT 18
Page 39-40

1. **PHRASES**
   a. with an injured leg (adj.)
   b. by the creek (adv.)
   c. of mine (adj.)
   d. of the children (adv.)
   e-f. Answers will vary.
2. **CONJUNCTIONS**
   a. Although they were born in Italy they speak English fluently.
   b. The butcher sharpened the knife before he cut up the meat.
   c. The singing stopped when the record player broke down.
3. **ABBREVIATIONS**
   a. establishment / established
   b. history c. Bachelor of Arts
   d. degree e. for example
   f. Queensland and Northern Territory Aerial Services
4. **POSSESSIVE**
   a. the pencil's mark
   b. the trees' leaves
   c. the children's efforts
5. **WORD STUDY**
   a. interfere b. intersect
   c. intercede d. intercept
   e. interject
   f-g. Answers will vary.
6. **CHALLENGE CORNER**
   Answers will vary.
7. **WORD USAGE**
   a. interference b. interception
   c. unconsciousness
   d. untidiness

PROVERBS
If you rush into things without thinking them through, you may spoil everything / waste time.

UNIT 19
Page 41-42

1. **PHRASES**
   a-b. Answers will vary.
   c. near the pond (adv.)
   of different colours (adj.)
   d. with great skill (adv.)
   with the inexperienced drivers (adj.)
   e-f. Answers will vary.
2. **CONJUNCTIONS**
   a. Jeff played his tape recorder while he did his homework.
   b. Because Jamie's homework was incomplete, he was given a detention.
   c. He continued walking until the sun began to set.
   d. After he completed the tennis match, he ate afternoon tea.
3. **WORD STUDY**
   a. construct
   b. instruct
   c. obstruct
4. **PROOF READING**
   a. "Where have you been?" Mother asked when I came home.
   b. "We've won!" cried Jane. "Now we can have a holiday."
5. **CHALLENGE CORNER**
   a. inexhaustible
   b. extraction
   c. unobstructed
   d-e. Answers will vary.
6. **DEGREES OF COMPARISON**
   a. prettier b. heaviest
   c. hotter

IDIOM
A person who discourages

UNIT 20
Page 43-44

1. **DEGREE OF COMPARISON**
   a. most b. more
   c. more d. most
2. **ABBREVIATIONS**
   a. milligram
   b. Honorary, Honourable
   c. French d. Brothers
   e. Proprietary f. Association
3. **WORD STUDY**
   a. spoilt, have spoilt, am spoiling.
   b. steadied, have steadied, am steadying
   c. sprung, have sprung, am springing
   d. specialty e. spoilage
   f. shadowy
   g. steadily
4. **SELECT-A-WORD**
   a. sprang b. stationary
   c. stationery d. special
   e. split f. startle
   g. steady h. spoil
5. **THESAURUS**
   Answers will vary.
6. **WORD USAGE**
   a. special
   b. sprang
   c. stationary
   d. stationery
   e. spoil
7. **CHALLENGE CORNER**
   a-b. Answers will vary.
   c. steadily d. speechless
   e. specialised f. startling
8. **ABSTRACT NOUNS**
   a. optimism b. beauty
   c. legible d. scour
   e. regal f. elusive
   g. voluntary

PROVERBS
If you haven't heard anything bad, you can still hope.

ANSWERS

UNIT 21
Page 45-46

1. **CLAUSES**
   a. This is the book (P) which I used. (A)
   b. She saw the car (P) which was in the yard. (A)
   c. Here is the money (P) that I owe you. (A)
   d. I saw the girl (P) whose bike was stolen. (A)
   e. The girl took the vase (P) that was on the table. (A)
   f-h. Answers will vary.
2. **RELATIVE PRONOUNS**
   a. that or which
   b. that or which
   c. who d. who
3. **WORD STUDY**
   a. reply b. reject
   c. revise d. reserve
   e. recapture f. recognise
   g. repel
4. **WORD USAGE**
   a. recently b. recover
   c. record d. rescuer
   e. recognise / recommend
5. **CHALLENGE CORNER**
   a-d. Answers will vary.
   e. revenue
   f. recipe
6. **PROOF READING**
   a. their attend property
   b. beginning manager helped

IDIOM
To have a drink

UNIT 22
Page 47-48

1. **PHRASES & CLAUSES**
   a. as her mother (P)
   b. which was very green (C)
   c. which was lost (C)
   d. in the forest (P)
   e. whom he met last week (C)
2. **ABBREVIATIONS**
   a. photo b. uni. c. mic.
   d. plane e. exam. f. hi-fi
3. **SPEECH**
   a. Tring boasted that he had collected twenty-two stickers.
   b. Mother complained as she came home that they had shopped all day and hadn't bought a thing.
   c. Maggie boasted, "I am a wonderful tennis player."
   d. Mina asked her teacher, "May I leave the room?"
4. **WORD STUDY**
   a. dangerous b. courageous
   c. mischievous d. glorious
5. **VERBS**
   a. replied, have replied, am replying
   b. rescued, have rescued am rescuing
6. **CHALLENGE CORNER**
   a. timetable b. friends/mates
   c. bulb d. tram e. petrol
   f. misery/caution/curiosity/anxiety
   g. horrific h. caution
   i. possibilities
7. **SELECT-A-WORD**
   a. possible b. valuable
   c. horrible d. anxious
   e. cautious f. vicious
   g. miserable

PROVERB
A person who is new to a position can make a fresh start.

UNIT 23
Page 49-50

1. **CLAUSES**
   a. We heard a loud scream (P) as we walked towards the haunted house. (A)
   b. We drove home (P) after the end of year concert was finished. (A)
   c. I catch the seven o'clock ferry (P) when I wake up early. (A)
   d. I can't afford a ticket (P) although I want to see the Pink Panthers. (A)
   e. We bought an ice cream during the intermission (P) while sitting in the foyer. (A)
2. **VOCABULARY**
   a. a waterhole in the creek
   b. an aborigine's hut of boughs and bark
   c. the bush; back country
   d. a goldminer; a tool
3. **LANGUAGE**
   a. monolith b. monarch
   c. dialogue d. microbe
   e. zoology f. micrometer
   g. ornithology
4. **SUFFIXES**
   a. excusable b. advisable
   c. manageable d. serviceable
5. **WORD STUDY**
   a. untidily b. uncommon
   c. invisible d. immortal
   e. irregular f. incurable
   g. unnecessary h. insincere
   i. cancellation j. accidental
   k. classification l. impatiently
   m.drawl n. drought
   o. drowse
6. **CHALLENGE CORNER**
   a. duplicate b. tolerate
   c. terminate d. interrogate
   e. accommodation f. classified
   g. accidental h. impatiently
   i-j. Answers will vary.
7. **SELECT-A-WORD**
   a. patients b. patience
   c. drawer d. draw

ANALOGIES
anvil

UNIT 24
Page 51-52

1. **CONTRACTIONS**
   a. Were not b. it would
   c. shall not d. will not
   e. who will f. cannot
   g. I would h. they have
   i. it'd j. wouldn't k. can't
   l. who'll; we've m. They've
   n. weren't o. shan't
2. **PUNCTUATION**
   a. "I've never seen him before!" exclaimed Tien.
   b. "What do you want the walking stick for?" asked the girl.
   c. baby's d. teachers'
   e. farmers'
3. **WORD STUDY**
   a. the study of animal life
   b. the study of a person's life
   c. geography
   d. geology
4. **WORD USAGE**
   a. autograph b. astronomy
   c. biography d. geometry
5. **SELECT-A-WORD**
   a. amphibious b. asterisk
   c. microphone
   d. stenographer
6. **CHALLENGE CORNER**
   a. biological b. geometric
   c. metric d. automatic
   e. lend f. loan
   g. past h. past
   i. past j. passed
   k. between l. among

IDIOM
To soothe strife with tact

ANSWERS

UNIT 25
Page 55-56

1. **PHRASES & CLAUSES**
   a. clause b. phrase
   c. phrase d. clause
   e. She spoke to the boy (P) who had a . . . (adj.)
   f. The ship started to sink (P) before the large . . . (adv.)
   g. The tennis player slipped (P) as he ran . . . (adv.)
   h. She was happy (P) when her mother gave . . . (adv.)
2. **ABBREVIATIONS**
   a. United Nations
   b. Video Cassette Recorder
   c. Central Business District
   d. Liquid Petroleum Gas
3. **WORD STUDY**
   a. employment b. ownership
   c. merriment d. contentment
   e. agreed, have agreed, am agreeing
   f. equipped, have equipped am equipping
   g. agreed, agreeable, disagree agreeing, agreement
   h. friendly, unfriendly, friendship, friendliness
4. **SELECT-A-WORD**
   a. argument b. achievement
   c. improvement
   d. equipment e. hardship
5. **HOMOPHONES**
   a. week b. weak c. whose
   d. Who's e. tide f. tied
6. **CHALLENGE CORNER**
   Answers will vary.
7. **PROOF READING**
   "Do you think we should go in there?" Jamie asked. "There is a notice which says that trespassers will be prosecuted." "We did agree that we would use our judgement," said Pete.

ANALOGIES
veal

UNIT 26
Page 57-58

1. **CONJUNCTIONS**
   a. The antidote was given immediately after the man was bitten by the snake.
   or After the man was bitten by the snake the antidote was given.
   b. Then/after c. although
   d. Because
2. **PRESENT PARTICIPLES**
   a. Noticing the smoke, he remembered . . .
   b. Coming home, she saw . . .
   c. Fishing one day, Jacob . . .
3. **WORD USAGE**
   a. contradict b. counterfeit
   c. antidote d. circumference
   e. antagonist
4. **WORD STUDY**
   a. circumnavigate
   b. circumstances
   c. circulate d. counterfeit
   e. contrast f. contrary
5. **CHALLENGE CORNER**
   a-d. Answers will vary.
   e. blacksmith
   f. caterer
   g. architect
6. **LANGUAGE**
   a. program
   b. diagonal
   c. Answers will vary.

ANALOGIES
bank

UNIT 27
Page 59-60

1. **CLAUSES**
   a. which bounced off the walls (adj.)
   b. after they had lit a fire (adv.)
   c. as the tide was rising (adv.)
   d-f. Answers will vary.
2. **SIMILES**
   a. lily b. rainbow c. crystal
   d. pancake e. lightning
   f. cucumber g. honey
   h. fire i. cat j. lark
   k. cricket l. bee
   m.mouse
3. **NOUNS**
   a. solving/solution
   b. distraction/distracting
   c. discussion/discussing
   d. division/dividing
   e. investigation/investigating
4. **THESAURUS**
   Answers will vary.
5. **WORD STUDY**
   a. distract b. divide
   c. discuss d. dissect
   e. dispel f. dislocate
   g. divert
6. **CHALLENGE CORNER**
   a. outdistance
   b. disappointment
   c. investigation d. undergrowth
   e-f. Answers will vary.
7. **PROOF READING**
   The disappointed teacher discussed the investigation. "I can't understand why the sugar did not dissolve and become invisible. We can divide and try again."

ANALOGIES chase

UNIT 28
Page 61-62

1. **PLURALS**
   a. passers-by
   b. maids of honour
   c. sons-in-law
   d. mothers-in-law
   e. courts-martial
   f. classes g. beauties
   h. suffixes i. yourselves
   j. guesses k. climaxes
   l. injuries m. kidneys
   n. thieves o. hangers-on
   p. heroes q. women
   r. There were some blue butterflies on the branches of the small bushes near the fences.
2. **SPEECH**
   a. Mother told Jane, "Put down your toys. It's your turn to do the washing-up."
   b. "We've blown a fuse," Mum stammered as she searched for the candles.
   c. The lifesaver warned that they should swim between the flags.
   d. Jane cried that she had lost her way home.
3. **WORD STUDY**
   a. misfortune b. unfortunate
   c. originally
   d. modernity/modernise
   e. dispossess f. worshipped
   g. Answers will vary.
   h. modernised, have modernised, am modernising
   i. worshipped, have worshipped, am worshipping
4. **WORD USAGE**
   a. occasional b. opportunity
   c. worshipped
5. **DICTIONARY WORK**
   a. lopsided b. nicotine c. petition
   d. evaporate e. bouquet
6. **CHALLENGE CORNER**
   a. improvise
   b. have a good trip
   c. first appearance
   d. and so on e. and the reverse
7. **SELECT-A-WORD**
   a. modern b. original
   c. ordinary
   d-f. Answers will vary.

ANALOGIES
Canada

ANSWERS

UNIT 29 Page 63-64

1. **LANGUAGE**
a. tractor b. contract
c. extract d. subtract
e. easily moved
f. introduce / bring in
g. fluid h. fluent
i. superfluous j. important
k. influence l. attraction

2. **WORD STUDY**
a. trans/port/a/tion
b. port/a/bil/ity
c. con/trac/tor
d. traverse e. translate
f. transcribe g. transfer

3. **EXTENSION WORDS**
Answers will vary

4. **PROOF READING**
a. porter's didn't
b. I'm
c. They're Katy's

5. **CLAUSES**
Answers will vary.

6. **CHALLENGE CORNER**
a. frequency above the human ear's audibility
b. forms of an element differing in weight of atoms
c. able to divide into new cells
d. particles falling after an explosion
e. Answers will vary.

7. **ABBREVIATIONS**
a. Limited b. permanent
c. Proprietary
d. distant/district
e. max. f. est. g. a.m.
h. approx.

8. **SELECT-A-WORD**
a. import b. export

IDIOM
She eats very little.

UNIT 30 Page 65-66

1. **CONTRACTIONS**
a. who've b. you're
c. didn't d. who's
e. will not f. are not
g. does not h. we're
i. you'll j. it's
k. shan't
l-m. Answers will vary.

2. **WORD STUDY**
a. electrify b. entertain
c. economise d. erode
e. elected

3. **WORD USAGE**
a. entertainment
b. electrician c. exercising
d. employment e. employer
f. education

4. **LANGUAGE**
a. telephone b. stereophonic
c. sympathy d. synchronise
e. phonics f. chronometer

5. **CHALLENGE CORNER**
a. platoon b. cartoon
c. tycoon d. typhoon
e. inexperienced
f. educational/experimental
g. electoral h. uneconomic

6. **SELECT-A-WORD**
a. enormous/electric
b. electric
c. economic/enormous

7. **VOCABULARY**
Answers will vary.

IDIOM
I felt I didn't belong or fit in.

UNIT 31 Page 67-68

1. **ALTERNATIVE WORDS**
Answers will vary.

2. **WORD STUDY**
a. dramatist b. geologist
c. organist d. vocalist
e. to make larger
f. to make simpler
g. to make more beautiful
h. successful i. painful

3. **CLAUSES**
a. Answers will vary.
b. because he had a tiring day. (adv.)
c. When the storm broke (adv.)
d. who lived near the river (adj.)
e. whom he met last week (adj.)

4. **PUNCTUATION**
a. Mr b. Prof. c. Rd
d. Wed. e. haven't f. she'll
g. "Have you read the 'Bridge to Terabithia' yet?" she asked.
h. "We've had enough!" she exclaimed.
i. "Where in Europe have you travelled?" he asked.
j. Mrs Lippa, the shopkeeper, was stacking the shelves.

5. **CHALLENGE CORNER**
a. unhappily b. untruthfully
c. unpurified d. mangrove
e. manage f. manoeuvre

6. **SELECT-A-WORD**
a. faithful b. florist
c. purify d. truthful
e. happiness f. purify

IDIOM
It will be easy.

UNIT 32 Page 69-70

1. **PUNCTUATION**
a. brother's man's
b. women's servant's
c. "My that's great!" exclaimed Jason. "Did you make it yourself?"
d. "Yes we can," warned the officer, "and we'll be back before sunset."
e. "Eva and Maria have done this!" exclaimed Adam.

2. **SELECT-A-WORD**
a. enemy b. necessary
c. dense d. sense

3. **PHRASES & CLAUSES**
a. They jumped from the tractor (Cl)
when it stopped (Cl)
b. The man was very hot (Cl)
in the jacket (Ph)
c. He could not walk any farther (Cl)
he was tired (Cl)
d. The river was filled with junk (Cl)
between the trees (Ph)
e. Suzanne borrowed a book (Cl)
she had nothing to read (Cl)

4. **WORD STUDY**
a. sensible b. vehicular
c. temperate d. misplace
e. misuse f. mislead
g. mispronounce
h. behaved, have behaved, am behaving
i. celebrated, have celebrated, am celebrating
j. densely k. necessarily

5. **WORD USAGE**
a. celebration b. vehicular
c. fertilise d. necessary/sensible
e. temperate f. dense

6. **CHALLENGE CORNER**
a. endure b. divide
c. prosper d. beautify
e. happiness f. republic
g. dissolve h. assist
i. converse j. extract

7. **PROOF READING**
bandage vehicle harbour
economic council/counsel
library sufficient excellent
marvellous manufacture

IDIOM
He is in trouble.

ALLPRINT

PRINTERS

&

GRAPHICS

Call us for all your printing needs:

- **Book printing and binding**
- **Office and personal stationery**
- **Advertising and brochures**
- **Artwork, typesetting and film work**

Great customer service

- ***Employer of qualified staff anxious to provide quality products***
- **Contact one of our assistants on (02) 557 3821**
- **Meet the showroom attendant near the security gate at the Lewin Street entrance**

YOU'LL BE IMPRESSED WITH THE QUALITY OF OUR SERVICE AND WORK

UNIT 10, 47 LEWIN ST, MALLORY

(02) 9557 3821

6. CORNER Challenge

Choose extension words.

a. a magnificent ________

b. an important ________

c. left ________

d. ________ land

e. ________ of the ancient kingdom

Find words to fit.

f.

5. Select-A-WORD

Choose list words

a. one who manages to avoid death ________

b. one who delivers a note ________

c. one who looks on ________

Choose antonyms from the list.

d. proprietor ________ e. tourist ________

f. employee ________ g. resident ________

Write words to match meanings.

h. An entertainer who earns money in the street ________

i. one who shoes horses ________

j. one who organises exhibitions ________

7. Dictionary Work

a. fos________ to search for gold

b. int________ to feel strongly

c. mor________ to cause embarrassment

d. pre________ to make ready

e. sch________ time table

f. dwi________ to gradually become smaller

g. hab________ can be lived in

Analogies. Husband is to wife as emperor is to ________

UNIT 18 Extension

interview	interrupt
intercept	interfere
outline	outcast
outrun	outlaw
unconscious	untidy
unfortunately	unhealthy
unconscious	unusual

interviewer
interruption
interference
outrage
outer
outsider
consciousness
untidiness
usually
unconsciousness

____

____

1. LOOKING AT adverbial & adjectival phrases

Adverbial phrases describe *how, when, where* or *why*.

e.g. The boy in the car is my brother.
(adjectival phrase)
The boy is in the car.
(adverbial phrase telling where)

Underline the phrases and write 'adjectival' or 'adverbial'.

a. Here is the horse with an injured leg.
☐ *adjectival* ☐ *adverbial*

b. Many of the children played by the creek.
☐ *adjectival* ☐ *adverbial*

c. That coat of mine is brand new.
☐ *adjectival* ☐ *adverbial*

d. Several of the children collected the books.
☐ *adjectival* ☐ *adverbial*

Use 'in the car' as an adjectival phrase and as an adverbial phrase.

e. ____

____

f. ____

____

2. CONJUNCTIONS

Join the sentences.

a. They speak English fluently.
They were born in Italy. (although)

____

____

b. The butcher sharpened the knife.
He cut up the meat. (before)

____

____

c. The singing stopped. (when)
The record player broke down.

____

____

3. ABBREVIATIONS

Write the full words.

a. estab. ________________________
b. hist. ________________________
c. B.A. ________________________
d. deg. ________________________
e. e.g. ________________________
f. QANTAS ________________________

4. POSSESSIVE

Add 's to singular and plural words.
<u>Exception:</u> If a word is plural and already ends with an s, add ' only.

e.g. the medal of the hero
— the hero's medal
the light of the candles
— the candles' light

a. the mark of a pencil

____

b. the leaves of the trees

____

c. the efforts of the children

____

"Forestdale Park"

THE STATE'S PREMIER NEW HOUSING DEVELOPMENT

Overlooking bush reserve and parklands
Executive living at its best

- Clever use of building and road construction does not interfere with the delightful undulating country.
- Choice positioning of homes does not interrupt the view over the Galen Valley.
- Charming homes of unusual but practical design have already been established.
- Breathe the pure mountain air, not an unhealthy smog-laden atmosphere.
- Waiting is unnecessary.

Telephone for an interview or consultation now!

(041) 712 5729

Nicole Kalligeror
or
Brandon Ladas

6. CORNER Challenge

Use these extension words in sentences.

a. | outsider | unusual |

____

____

____

b. | unfortunately | interruption |

____

____

____

c. | interviewer | interference |

____

____

____

d. | outer | unconsciousness |

____

____

____

5. WORD STUDY

The prefix 'inter' means 'between'.

e.g. an interview
— a discussion between two people

Match words to meanings.

a. to meddle or oppose
b. where two lines cross
c. to go between, on behalf of another
d. to stop a moving thing
e. to interrupt

intercede
intercept
interject
intersect
interfere

Add prefixes and suffixes to build word families.

f. | health | ______________________

____

g. | tidy | ______________________

____

7. word usage

Change list words to nouns and complete.

a. Because of his i__________ they were late starting the project.

b. The __________ of the message meant there was no surprise attack.

c. The patient lapsed into u__________ during the day.

d. The __________ of her room was legendary.

Proverbs. Explain 'Haste makes waste' ______________________

UNIT 19

exceed	expose
exhaust	extract
extinct	examine
especially	eventually
ancestor	excessive
structure	construct
instruct	obstruct

Extension

exhaustion
inexhaustible
extraction
re-examined
specifically
specialty
specialisation
ancestral
constructive
unobstructed

____

____

1. LOOKING AT phrases

Add phrases as indicated.

a. Some boys *(adjectival)* ________________ ______________ walked quickly *(adverbial)* ______________________________.

b. *(adverbial)* ________________________ the colt galloped *(adverbial)* ____________ ______________________________.

Underline the phrases, indicating whether they are adjectival or adverbial.

c. Near the pond were small shrubs of different colours.

d. With great skill the champion driver overtook the cars with the inexperienced drivers.

Use 'by the door' as an adverbial and an adjectival phrase.

e. *(adverbial)* ______________________________

____

f. *(adjectival)* ______________________________

____

2. LOOKING AT conjunctions

Choose a word to join the sentences.

because	while	
although	until	after

a. Jeff played his tape recorder. He did his homework.

____

____

____

b. Jamie's homework was incomplete. Jamie was given a detention.

____

____

____

c. He continued walking. The sun began to set.

____

____

____

d. He completed the tennis match. He ate afternoon tea.

____

____

____

3. WORD STUDY

The Latin root 'struo' means 'I build'.

e.g. structure — that which is built

Choose list words.

a. to build together

____

b. to provide instruction

____

c. to build or place in the way

____

PART 1

WHITEWASHING THE FENCE

Characters: Aunt Polly, Tom, Ben Rogers, Billy Fisher, Narrator.

Narrator: It is a beautiful summer day as Tom, carrying a large pail of whitewash and a long-handled brush, is hurried out of the shed by Aunt Polly.

Aunt Polly: (stops, points at fence) Here, Tom, this will do. I want the fence whitewashed, boy. (pause) You must <u>eventually</u> learn right from wrong.

Tom: (sadly) Please, Aunt Polly, wouldn't a licking do as well?

Aunt Polly: (seriously) I'm sure you'd <u>especially</u> like something else but I know this is a better punishment for you, Tom. You may take heed when I tell you not to run away from school. You can <u>exhaust</u> yourself here today.

Tom: (in a whining voice) Aw, please, Aunt Polly.

Aunt Polly: (seriously) No, Tom, I've made up my mind. (pause) You do the job and don't leave 'til it's all done or I'll skin you alive, do you hear?

Aunt Polly leaves. Tom <u>examines</u> the <u>structure</u>, dips brush into whitewash – paints two strokes – looks at rest of fence and sits down sadly on log.

... *continued on Page 44*

5. CORNER Challenge

Choose extension words.

a. There seemed to be an __________ supply of coal in the vast deposits.

b. The __________ of the minerals from rocks was a different process.

c. The people had an __________ view of the show.

Explain the difference in meaning.

d. | stature | statue |

____

____

____

e. | intolerable | intolerant |

____

____

____

4. Proof Reading

Rewrite adding capitals, inverted commas, commas, question marks, full stops and exclamation marks.

a. where have you been mother asked when I came home

____

____

b. we've won cried jane now we can have a holiday

____

____

6. Degrees of Comparison

e.g. Our guest was late. *(one)*
My dad came home later *(two)*
but my grandfather arrived latest.
(three or more)

Write the correct degree of comparison.

a. Margaret is pretty but her sister is (pretty)__________.

b. That bag is the (heavy)__________ I have picked up.

c. Today is (hot)__________ than yesterday.

Idiom. Explain 'a wet blanket' ______________________

UNIT 20 Extension

special	split
spoil	spoken
sprang	square
shadow	shrub
startle	stationary
steady	stationery
stomach	whitewashing

specialised
speaker
speech
speechless
shadowy
shrubbery
startling
unsteady
steadily
steadiness
____
____

1. LOOKING AT degrees of comparison

e.g. Jack is small. *(one person)*
Jean is smaller. *(comparing two people)*
Meg is the smallest in the group. *(more than two)*

Many words need 'more/less' for the comparative and 'most/least' when comparing more than two.

e.g. beautiful — more/less beautiful
most/least beautiful

Write the correct form.

a. Of all the cars in the show this is the __________ attractive.
b. She was always __________ careful than her sister.
c. They always spoke __________ clearly than their friends.
d. Of all the tracks in the yard this is the __________ dangerously overloaded.

2. ABBREVIATIONS

Write the full word.

a. mg __________ b. Hon. __________
c. Fr. __________ d. Bros __________
e. Pty __________ f. Ass'n __________

3. WORD STUDY

e.g. ring —
rang have rung am ringing

Write the three parts of these verbs.

a. spoil __________ __________ __________
b. steady __________ __________ __________
c. spring __________ __________ __________

Add these suffixes.

age	ty	y	ily

d. special_____ e. spoil_____
f. shadow_____ g. steady_____

4. Select-A-WORD

a. The animal __________ from the bushes. (sprang, sprung)
b. The __________ truck was parked beside the road. (stationery, stationary)
c. They bought the __________ from the newsagent. (stationery, stationary)

Choose synonyms from the list.

d. exceptional __________
e. divide __________
f. disturb __________
g. firm __________
h. ruin __________

5. Thesaurus

Find synonyms.

a. inspect __________
b. display __________
c. remove __________
d. extreme __________

WHITEWASHING THE FENCE

Tom: (speaking to himself) I sure wish I had something to swap with the boys so they'd help me do the whitewashing. (He feels in his pockets.) No, nothing of much use there. (long pause) This will really spoil my day.
(quietly to himself) Yes, yes, that could be the way.

Tom picks up a brush and begins to work.
Ben Rogers enters.

Ben: (smiling) Hullo! Hullo! Poor old Tom's at work.

Tom: (quietly but not sadly) Oh, hullo, Ben. (Tom continues whitewashing.)

Ben: Poor old Tom has to work while I'm going swimming. (Ben chuckles.) But I suppose you like to work on holidays, eh Tom? (Tom continues whitewashing.)

Tom: (quietly) If you call this work I think I'd rather be here. It's special.
(quietly while still whitewashing) You heard right, Ben. (pause)
(Tom brushes carefully and adds a touch here and there.) Not everybody could do this fence properly. Steady skill is needed.

... continued on Page 46

7. CORNER Challenge

Explain the difference in meaning.

a. | symbol | cymbal |

____

____

____

b. | profit | prophet |

____

____

____

Choose extension words.

c. walked ___________ forward

d. ___________ with anger

e. ___________ in creating ornaments

f. ___________ sounds

6. word usage

Choose list words.

a. All the people gathered for the ___________ event.

b. The huge animal ___________ across the ground from the thicket.

c. The ___________ train had been at the platform for fifteen minutes.

d. Will you purchase all the ___________ at the newsagent?

e. The food will ___________ if it is not refrigerated.

8. Abstract Nouns

Form abstract nouns from the underlined words.

a. An optimistic person is known for his ___________.

b. A beautiful woman is known for her ___________.

Match words and phrases.

c. able to be read
d. to scrub
e. suitable for a king
f. difficult to catch
g. done for no payment

scour
regal
legible
voluntary
elusive

Proverbs. Explain 'No news is good news' ___________________________

UNIT 21 Extension

recent	record
recover	regard
regular	recipe
replied	rescue
revenue	recognise
recommend	represent
rectangular	restaurant

recently
recoveries
regulate
irregularly
regulations
rescuer
unrecognisable
recognition
recommendation
representative

____

____

1. LOOKING AT *adjectival clauses*

The main thought in a sentence is the principal clause. A clause has a verb and a subject. An adjectival clause describes the subject.

The trees, which are bare, make the garden stark.

principal clause — *adjectival clause* — *principal clause*

Underline the principal and adjectival clauses as above.

a. This is the book which I used.
b. She saw the car which was in the yard.
c. Here is the money that I owe you.
d. I saw the girl whose bike was stolen.
e. The girl took the vase that was on the table.

Use 'which I bought' as an adjectival clause.

f. ______________________________________

____

Add adjectival clauses.

g. The animal ______________________________
is in the paddock.

h. Have you seen the toy ______________________

____

2. LOOKING AT *relative pronouns*

Remember:
who or **whom** for **people**
which or **that** for **animals** and **objects**

Join the sentences using the correct pronoun.

a. The plant is growing in the pot.
It is climbing ivy.

____

____

____

b. Jacqui sat on the bed.
She found was broken.

____

____

____

c. Geoff telephoned his boss. He was unable to attend the party.

____

____

____

d. I spoke to my brother.
He ran up the stairs.

____

____

____

3. WORD STUDY

The prefix 're' means 'back or again'.

e.g. recover — to get something back

Match words and meanings.

a. to answer
b. to not accept
c. to re-read
d. to keep back
e. to catch again
f. to identify
g. to drive back

recapture
reply
recognise
reject
repel
revise
reserve

WHITEWASHING THE FENCE

Ben: (quickly) Bet I could. (pause) Here, let me try.

Tom: (quietly, still whitewashing) Afraid not, Ben. Aunt Polly's very particular about the fence. I guess I'm just about the only boy who can do it the way Aunt Polly wants it. (Tom continues whitewashing.)

Ben: (eagerly) Oh! Come on, Tom.

Tom: No, I'm sorry, Ben. It just can't be done. Aunt Polly wouldn't recommend it.

Ben: (seriously) Now see here, Tom, let me try. (pause) Look, I'll give you the core of my apple.

Tom: (seriously) Well, alright, Ben. (pause) No, Ben I'd better not.

Ben: Oh, come on, Tom! (pause) I'll give you all the apple!

Tom: Well, I will, Ben. (stops whitewashing) But be very careful. Make the strokes regular.

Ben gives Tom the apple and starts working slowly and carefully. Tom sits down to eat the apple.
Billy Fisher enters with a kite in his hand.

Billy: (smiling) You working, Ben? (pause) Don't you know it's Saturday.

Ben: (quickly) Go away, Billy! I'm busy! I don't regard this as real work. (Ben continues whitewashing.)

Billy: (smiling) Busy on Saturday? That'll be a record for you.

... continued on Page 48

4. word usage

Choose list and extension words.

a. Just __________ we have been able to travel on the new road.

b. The patient did not __________ from the illness for a week.

c. The company will __________ the number of tonnes of metal extracted.

d. The __________ of the twins was given an award for bravery.

e. The salesperson said that she did not __________ the design.

5. CORNER Challenge

These words mean 'main':

principal central prime supreme important

Write a phrase showing how the word can best be used.

e.g. principal area for investment

a. central __________

b. prime __________

c. supreme __________

d. important __________

Choose list words.

e. money collected by governments __________

f. a set of directions for making something __________

6. Proof Reading

Rewrite incorrect spelling.

a. Did thier friends atend the school on that propertey?

b. In the begining the maneger helpped the new workers.

____

Idiom. Explain 'to wet one's whistle' __________

UNIT 22 Extension

possible	impossible
horrible	accessible
miserable	valuable
anxious	comfortable
cautious	various
vicious	furious
curious	marvellous

possibilities
horrify
horrific
misery
valueless
uncomfortably
anxiety
caution
curiosity
marvelled

____

____

1. LOOKING AT phrases & clauses

Jacqui wore a dress with blue stripes.
(adjectival phrase – no verb)
Jim who was hunting rabbits searched the hillside.
(adjectival clause – 'was hunting' – verb)

Adjectival clauses begin with 'where', 'when', 'who', 'whom', 'whose', 'which', 'that' or 'as'.

Underline the phrase or clause. Write which it is.

a. That calf is the same colour as her mother.
   ❑ *phrase* ❑ *clause*

b. Two creeks flowed through the valley which was very green. ❑ *phrase* ❑ *clause*

c. The deer which was lost was found yesterday.
   ❑ *phrase* ❑ *clause*

d. The boy, in the forest, noticed the smoke.
   ❑ *phrase* ❑ *clause*

e. He hoped to see the girl whom he met last week.
   ❑ *phrase* ❑ *clause*

2. ABBREVIATIONS

e.g. influenza — flu

a. photograph ______ b. university ______

c. microphone ______ d. aeroplane ______

e. examination ______ f. high fidelity ______

3. Direct & Indirect Speech

Direct speech is what is actually spoken.

e.g. "I've jumped over the creek!" she yelled.

Indirect speech is reported speech.

e.g. She yelled that she had jumped over the creek.

Write as indirect speech.

a. "I have collected twenty-two stickers," boasted Tring.

____

b. Mother complained as she came home, "We shopped all day and didn't buy a thing."

____

Write as direct speech.

c. Maggie boasted that she was a wonderful tennis player.

____

d. Mina asked her teacher for permission to leave the room.

____

4. WORD STUDY

Write words ending in 'ous' to match the meanings.

a. full of danger ______

b. full of courage ______

c. full of mischief ______

d. full of glory ______

WHITEWASHING THE FENCE

Tom: (seriously) Well, it's not exactly being busy at work, Billy. (pause) It's impossible for most people to do this properly. Ben here seems like a good hand with a brush – he gave me an apple to have a chance at doing it.

Ben: (continuing whitewashing) That's right, Billy, not everybody can do it. Takes skill. Have to be cautious about who does this.

Billy: (eagerly) It does, eh! (pause) Well, give me a try. I'm curious.

Tom: (quietly) No, I don't think so, Billy, we don't need any help. (A long pause. Tom looks at fence.) Say, that's a fine kite you've got there, Billy!

Billy: She's a good one, alright, Tom. Valuable too. (pause, then says excitedly) Say! I'll tell you what! I'll give it to you if you let me whitewash a little.

Tom: (slowly) Well, I don't know, Billy, but I...I... (pause) Well, alright. Ben looks a bit tired there.

Narrator: Tom's working day turned out to be comfortable and profitable. The boys paid various articles for the honour of performing the task. Tom discovered that, to make someone wish for something, it is necessary to make it hard to get.

6. CORNER Challenge

Some American words have equivalent words in Australian English.

e.g. sidewalk — footpath

Write the Australian terms.

a. schedule (train) ____________

b. buddies ____________

c. globe (light) ____________

d. streetcar ____________

e. gasoline ____________

Choose extension words.

f. full of ____________

g. an ____________ accident

h. proceed with ____________

i. many different ____________

5. LOOKING AT verbs

Write the three parts.

e.g.	record	*(present tense)*
	recorded	*(past tense)*
	have recorded	*(past participle)*
	am recording	*(present participle)*

a. reply ____________

____________ ____________

b. rescue ____________

____________ ____________

7. Select-A-WORD

Choose antonyms from the list.

a. unlikely ____________

b. worthless ____________

c. pleasant ____________

d. relaxed ____________

e. careless ____________

f. gentle ____________

g. cheerful ____________

Proverb. 'A new broom sweeps clean' ____________

UNIT 23 Extension

accommodate	indicated
accompany	accident
activity	aborigine
candidate	cancel
calendar	classify
drawer	patient
savage	variety

unaccompanied
accidental
inactively
accommodation
cancellation
classified
classification
impatience
impatiently
savagery
____
____

1. LOOKING AT adverbial clauses

The main thought is the principal clause.
An adverbial clause tells how, when, where or why.
A clause has a verb.

e.g. The children walked away because it was late.
principal clause — *adverbial clause (why)*

Underline the principal and adverbial clauses as above.

a. As we walked towards the haunted house, we heard a loud scream.
b. We drove home after the end of year concert was finished.
c. I catch the seven o'clock ferry when I wake up early.
d. Although I want to see The Pink Panthers, I can't afford a ticket.
e. We bought an icecream during the intermission while sitting in the foyer.

2. Vocabulary

Explain these words.

a. billabong _______________
b. gunyah _______________
c. mulga _______________
d. digger _______________

3. LOOKING AT language

These words were derived from Greek

monos — alone
e.g. monarch, monolith, monologue, monotonous
logus means a **talk** or **discourse**
e.g. ornithology, dialogue, epilogue, geology, zoology
mikvos means **small**
e.g. microbe, micrometer microscope

Choose words.

a. The huge stone ___________ stood out in the centre of the desert.
b. The young prince was made the ___________ of the kingdom.
c. When she began reading the ___________ of the play, she found it interesting.
d. The scientists examined the ___________ with a microscope.
e. The study of animal life ___________
f. An instrument for measuring very small objects ___________
g. The study of bird life ___________

4. adding Suffixes

If a word ends in 'e', the 'e' is usually left off when the suffixes 'able' or 'ible' are used.

e.g. sense — sensible

If the words ends in 'ce' or 'ge' do <u>not</u> drop the 'e'.

e.g. change — changeable

a. excuse ___________
b. advise ___________
c. manage ___________
d. service ___________

Thursday, July 7th

Today our group visited Ellsmere. I was really looking forward to the science centre activity lab.

We enjoyed the bus trip, joking and laughing all the way. Miss Jackson was supposed to accompany us, but she couldn't make it.

The cabins we are in accommodate eight. I am sharing with Marcia and our friends.

In the afternoon we read some science notes. I can't wait to try the wide variety of activities and displays. I hope no one has an accident.

The science buffs can't wait for tomorrow. Miss Foyer told them to be patient.

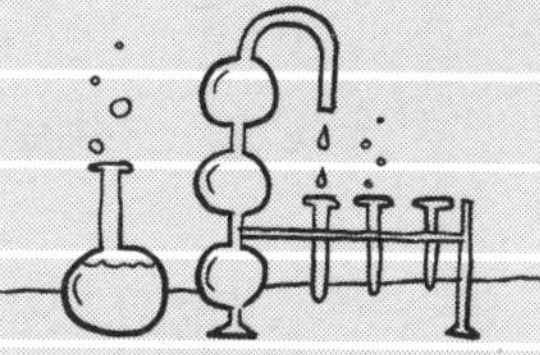

5. WORD STUDY

The prefixes 'un', 'im', 'in', 'il' and 'ir' all mean 'not' or 'the opposite of'.

e.g. pure — impure

Add prefixes.

a. ____tidily b. ____common
c. ____visible d. ____mortal
e. ____regular f. ____curable
g. ____necessary h. ____sincere

Add suffixes.

i. cancel______ j. accident______
k. classific______ l. impatient______

Add the blend 'dr'

m. ____awl n. ____ought o. ____owse

6. CORNER Challenge

Complete the ATE words.

a. to make a copy of something ___________
b. to put up with ___________
c. to finish with something completely ___________
d. to question very thoroughly ___________

Add extension words.

e. first-class ___________
f. ___________ information
g. ___________ damage
h. waiting ___________

Build words.

i. act ___________
____
____

j. company ___________
____
____

7. Select-A-WORD

a. The ___________ waited in the reception area. (patients, patience)
b. The boy showed a lot of ___________ to complete the puzzle. (patients, patience)
c. The ___________ in the cupboard would not open. (draw, drawer)
d. Did she ___________ the prize-winning sketch? (draw, drawer)

Analogies. Surgeon is to scalpel as blacksmith is to _______________.

UNIT 24

biology	biography
microbe	geology
geography	geometry
microscope	periscope
telescope	autograph
paragraph	graphic
astronomy	astrology

Extension

biological
autobiographical
microscopic
geometric
metric
micrometer
telegraphy
telephonist
automatic
astronomical

____

____

1. LOOKING AT contractions

An apostrophe ' is used when abbreviating or shortening words. It shows where letters have been left out.

Write in full.

a. weren't ___________ b. it'd ___________

c. shan't ___________ d. won't ___________

e. who'll ___________ f. can't ___________

g. I'd ___________ h. they've ___________

Write the abbreviation.

i. (It would) ___________ be good to know the reason.

j. It (would not) ___________ take long.

k. You (cannot) ___________ go in the deep end.

l. (Who will) ___________ know where (we have) ___________ gone?

m. (They have) ___________ gone away for the weekend.

n. You (were not) ___________ at the soccer match.

o. I (shall not) ___________ ask again.

2. LOOKING AT punctuation

Add all marks including quotation marks.

a. ive never seen him before exclaimed Tien.

____

____

b. what do you want the walking stick for asked the girl

____

____

____

Add apostrophes to show ownership.

Add 's to singular and plural words but if a plural word ends with an 's', only add '.

e.g. the bicycle of the boy — the boy's bike.
the bicycles of the boys — the boys' bikes.

c. the cry of a baby

____

d. the jobs of the teachers

____

e. the crops of the farmers

____

3. WORD STUDY

These words are derived from Greek.

'bios' means life.

Explain these words.

a. biology ___________________

b. biography ___________________

'geo' means the earth.

Write the words.

c. study of countries of the earth

____

d. study of rocks and minerals

____

Friday, July 8th

It was as exciting as we expected. We arrived at the science centre at 9:30 a.m. A guide explained that all the displays were on the first floor, and the hands-on activities on the second floor.

The astronomy display used special effects lighting to show stars and planets. The movement of the circular dome overhead made it realistic. The graphic geology display also used special effects to show how faulting, folding and volcanic activity take place.

After lunch all sorts of activities were set up on the second floor. We used computers, worksheets and cards. Microscopes and telescopes were for measuring and problem solving.

We can't wait to come back for a second visit.

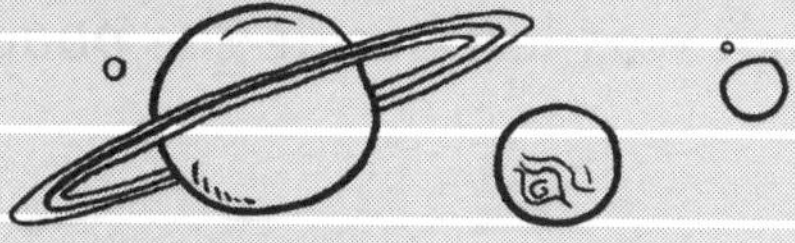

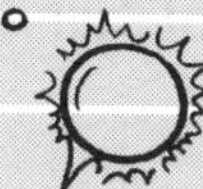

4. word usage

Choose list words.

a. The signature of a person is called an __________.

b. The study of stars and planets is known as __________.

c. The life of someone as told by another is a __________.

d. The study of lines in space is called __________.

5. Select-A-WORD

Choose a word from the same Greek root.

a. bios __________

b. aster __________

c. micros __________

d. grapho __________

amphibious
microphone
asterisk
stenographer

6. CORNER Challenge

Choose extension words.

a. __________ warfare

b. __________ shapes

c. __________ measures

d. __________ washer

Use in sentences.

loan — *noun*
lend — *verb*

e. She will __________ her book.

f. Can you give me a __________ of that instrument?

past — *adjective, noun, preposition*
passed — *verb*

g. It was written in the __________ tense.

h. The old man lives in the __________.

i. Do not go __________ the shop.

j. We __________ the new office building.

between *(two people)*
among *(more than two)*

k. It was shared __________ Rhonda and Sandra.

l. The cake was shared out __________ the children.

Idiom. Explain 'to pour oil on troubled waters' __________

REVIEW

Term 3

1. Choose the word that fits.

structure
telescope
eventually
biography
spectator
furious
attendant
accessible
represent

a. The ___________ had a good view of the basketball game.

b. The car park ___________ drove the car down the steep ramp.

c. The huge ___________ had been built by the Aztecs.

d. The ___________ wind blew across the ocean.

e. The old sailor used the ___________ to watch the ships.

f. The ___________ of the famous writer was interesting.

g. After cyclonic rains the beach was not ___________ for three weeks.

h. She ___________ discovered that her watch was left beside the pool.

2. Change these words to nouns.

a. announce ___________ c. exhaust ___________ e. possible ___________

b. interrupt ___________ d. regular ___________ f. recommend ___________

3. Change these words to adjectives.

a. exceed ___________ c. shadow ___________ e. microscope ___________

b. employ ___________ d. horror ___________ f. accident ___________

4. Underline and rewrite incorrectly spelt words.

a. It was unusuel for him to work undtidy. ___________

b. He was in reguler attender at the employmint agency. ___________

c. The survivers seaid that the perescope was seen a hundred metres away. ___________

d. It was such a miserible day the reguler games had to be postponce. ___________

5. Rewrite the sentences correctly.

a. Hav you scene the colours of the spectrum?

____

b. Did she captur the beuty of the countre seen?

____

c. After a long journy they found theirselves betwen two mountins.

____

d. She asked what was the prise of a cieling fan.

____

e. The sparkel of the cleer water cood be seen across the levil sand.

____

6. Choose a word.

a. The boy will __________ himself in the long race. (extract, exhaust)

b. The box of __________ was at the newsagent. (stationery, stationary)

c. The __________ on the right side of the cupboard was damaged. (draw, drawer)

d. They will __________ out the wet clothes. (ring, wring)

7. Write three nouns ending with any of these suffixes.

ar	er	or

__________ __________ __________

8. Write word families of at least 6 words of these.

a. heal ______________________________

b. tidy ______________________________

9. Write the three parts of these words.

a. steady __________ __________ __________

b. spring __________ __________ __________

10. Add the suffix 'able' or 'ible' to these words.

a. miser __________ c. sense __________

b. change __________ d. comfort __________

UNIT 25 Extension

achievement	agreement
amusement	instrument
government	argument
parliament	equipment
refreshment	judgement
improvement	hardship
advertisement	friendship

achiever
agreeable
instrumental
argumentative
governor
parliamentary
re-equipped
misjudge
friendliness
hard-earned

____

____

1. LOOKING AT phrases & clauses

Write whether they are phrases or clauses.

a. Because the pitch was waterlogged we could not play. ❑ *phrase* ❑ *clause*

b. Because of the drought the cattle died. ❑ *phrase* ❑ *clause*

c. Before the huge explosion the building was undamaged. ❑ *phrase* ❑ *clause*

d. Before we left he filled the water bottles. ❑ *phrase* ❑ *clause*

Underline the principal clause and double underline the adjectival or adverbial clauses.

e.g. I walked to the shop which was in the next street.

e. She spoke to the boy who had a new bicycle.

f. The ship started to sink before the large wave struck.

g. The tennis player slipped as he ran to the net.

h. She was happy when her mother gave her a new dress.

2. ABBREVIATIONS

Write in full.

a. U.N. ____________________

b. V.C.R. ____________________

c. C.B.D. ____________________

d. L.P.G. ____________________

3. WORD STUDY

The suffixes 'ment' and 'ship' mean 'state of being'.

e.g. friendship — state of being a friend
amusement — state of being happy or amused

Use these suffixes to build words.

a. state of being employed __________

b. state of being an owner __________

c. state of being merry __________

d. state of being content __________

Write the 3 verb parts.

e. agree __________ __________ __________

f. equip __________ __________ __________

Build words by adding prefixes and suffixes.

g. agree ________________ ________________

h. friend ________________ ________________

4. Select-A-WORD

Choose synonyms from the list.

a. disagreement __________

b. accomplishment __________

c. advancement __________

d. supplies __________

e. difficulty __________

Home-made Spring Balance

Equipment for the instrument:

- 1 round empty tin 8cm in diameter
- string
- nail (large)
- flat piece of timber 30cm long and 20cm wide
- pole approximately 30cm long
- rubber bands
- 50g and 100g weights

Methods:

- Punch 4 holes with the large nail around the edge of the tin.
- Pass pieces of string through the holes and tie them together.
- Attach the pole (C) to the flat piece of timber (B)
- Suspend the rubber band off the nail inserted 3cm from the top of the pole (D).
- Tie the four strings to the rubber band at A.
- Use the 50g and 100g weights to help you calibrate (mark the scale) on upright (C).
- You have created an effective 'spring balance' which is an improvement on guessing.

6. CORNER Challenge

Explain the difference in meaning.

a. | calendar | colander |

____

____

b. | forecast | foretell |

____

____

c. | council | counsel |

____

____

d. | statue | statute |

____

____

e. | industrial | industrious |

____

____

5. LOOKING AT homophones

| weak | week |

a. Last __________ we went to Ballina.

b. That sick old dog is very __________.

| who's | whose |

c. I do not know __________ book has been left behind.

d. "__________ taking those pencils away?" she asked.

| tide | tied |

e. The __________ will be high by six o'clock.

f. The launch was __________ up at the pier.

7. Proof Reading

Add punctuation.

do you think we should go in there jamie asked there is a notice which says that trespassers will be prosecuted we did agree that we would use our judgment said pete

____

____

____

____

____

Analogies. Mutton is to lamb as beef is to ______________.

UNIT 26 Extension

circumference	contradict
circumstances	antidote
counterfeit	antiseptic
antagonist	diagonal
diagram	dialogue
diameter	program
prologue	prophecy

circumstantial
contradictory
contrasting
anticyclone
antipathy
antique
antagonism
dialect
protractor
protrude

____

____

1. LOOKING AT conjunctions

Conjunctions join single words, phrases and clauses. They are used at the beginning or in the middle of the sentence.

e.g. She will leave early <u>because</u> she is tired.
<u>Because</u> she is tired, she will leave early.

Join the sentences using a conjunction.

a. The antidote was given immediately.
The man was bitten by the snake.

____

____

b. He measured the circumference and diameter.
He drew a diagram.

____

____

c. The dinosaur appeared on the program.
The model of the dinosaur was incomplete.

____

____

d. He was elated.
The surf was perfect for bodysurfing.

____

____

2. Present Participles

This is an interesting way to start a sentence.

e.g. When the car <u>turned</u> a corner, it burst a tyre. *(past tense)*
<u>Turning</u> a corner, the car burst a tyre. *(present participle)*

Rewrite the sentences, changing the underlined verbs to the present tense.

a. As he <u>noticed</u> the smoke, he remembered the devastation of the bush fires.

____

____

____

b. As she came home, she saw the gate was unlocked.

____

____

____

c. When Jacob fished one day, he caught a shoe.

____

____

____

3. word usage

Choose list words.

a. To argue an opposing view is to __________ someone.

b. Currency which is not produced by the government is called __________.

c. Medicine which acts against a poison is called an __________.

d. The distance around a circle is called the __________.

e. One opposed to you is an __________.

PART 1

The Spirit in the Tree

In the far off land called Befes there lived a king who had a magnificent palace.

One morning on a walk through the forest he came across the largest tree he had ever seen. The circumference measured seventy paces.

"Never have I seen a tree with such a huge diameter," he said in amazement. "I will use this tree to make a new palace."

The king ordered woodcutters to begin the task. The woodcutters wanted to protest but they could not contradict their king. The townspeople were alarmed by the king's command. The old prophecy stating that the town would be in danger if the tree was harmed struck fear in their hearts.

... continued on Page 60

5. CORNER Challenge

Explain these occupations.

a. domestic __________

b. glazier __________

c. chauffeur __________

d. auditor __________

Name the occupations.

e. makes things with iron for horses and farm work __________

f. provides food for parties and functions __________

g. designs buildings __________

4. WORD STUDY

The prefix 'circum' means 'round' or 'about'.

Match words and meanings.

a. to sail around

b. conditions around a particular event

c. go round

circumstances
circulate
circumnavigate

The prefix 'contra' means 'against'.

e.g. contradict — to say something against another

d. made in imitation

e. to show differences

f. opposite in position

contrast
contrary
counterfeit

6. LOOKING AT language

The Greek prefix 'dia' means 'through'.

e.g. diameter — through the centre of a circle

The prefix 'pro' means 'before'.

e.g. prophecy — foretelling the future

Name these.

a. a schedule of a performance __________

b. a line drawn from one corner of a shape to the opposite corner __________

Find four words beginning with prefix 'anti'.

c. __________ __________ __________ __________

Analogies. Tea is to caddy as money is to __________.

UNIT 27 Extension

disease	distant
dissolve	distrust
discuss	divide
disappointed	invisible
investigate	undermined
underground	underpay
underweight	underworld

outdistance
solvable
resolution
retractable
divisor
disappointment
visibility
investigation
understanding
undergrowth

____

____

1. LOOKING AT clauses

Adverbial clauses tell how, when, where or why. They begin with conjunctions.

e.g. They came when they heard of the plan.

principal clause *adverbial clause*

The gypsies who live in the village play the violins passionately.

adjectival clause

Underline the clauses and name them.

a. The echo, which bounced off the walls, sounded hollowly. ___________
b. The guides pitched their tents after they had lit a fire. ___________
c. He was in despair as the tide was rising round him. ___________

Add adverbial clauses.

d. She went to the stove when ______________ ____.
e. Because ________________________________ ________________ she did not collect the fruit.
f. He worked as if ________________________ ____

2. Similes

One thing is compared to another using words like 'like' or 'as'.

Match these.

rainbow lily crystal cucumber honey pancake lightning fire

a. as white as a ___________
b. as colourful as a ___________
c. as clear as ___________
d. as flat as a ___________
e. as quick as ___________
f. as cool as a ___________
g. as sweet as ___________
h. as hot as ___________

Complete.

i. as agile as a ___________
j. as happy as a ___________
k. as lively as a ___________
l. as busy as a ___________
m. as quiet as a ___________

3. LOOKING AT nouns

Write these words as nouns.

e.g. disappoint — the disappointment of

a. solve ___________
b. distract ___________
c. discuss ___________
d. divide ___________
e. investigate ___________

4. Thesaurus

Find synonyms.

a. incidents ___________
b. opponent ___________
c. schedule ___________
d. imitation ___________

PART 2

The Spirit in the Tree

From distant regions woodcutters came to town. Some believed if the giant tree was felled a terrible disease or plague would fall upon the town.

When the woodcutters went to the palace to talk to the king, the king refused to discuss it.

The disappointed people gathered at the base of the tree and decorated it with flowers.

Their leader, a woodcutter named Shahim, spoke to the tree. "Great invisible spirit of the tree, the plans to cut you down have been made. We have tried to stop this but without success. You must visit the king and prevent this disaster happening."

... continued on Page 62

5. WORD STUDY

The prefixes 'dis', 'dif' and 'di' means 'away' or 'apart'. Write the words.

a. to draw attention away from __________

b. to separate into parts __________

c. to talk about __________

Use these words.

dislocate	dispel	dissect	divert

d. The scientists will __________ the animal.

e. He tried to __________ the rumours by stating the facts.

f. Did she __________ her arm in the accident?

g. The townspeople tried to __________ the flood waters.

6. CORNER Challenge

Choose extension words.

a. The gazelle quickly began to __________ her pursuers.

b. It was a __________ when we missed the concert.

c. The police __________ took four months.

d. There hiding in the dense __________ was a deer.

Explain the difference between these pairs of words.

e. | aggravate | anticipate |

____

____

f. | persecute | prosecute |

____

____

7. Proof Reading

Rewrite with correct punctuation and spelling.

the disapointed teacher discused the investigation i can't understand why the sugar did not discolve and become inviseble we can divid and try again

____

____

____

____

____

Analogies. Unlawful is to illegal as pursuit is to __________.

UNIT 28 Extension

position	possess
foreign	fortunate
groceries	homestead
horizon	modern
mosquito	worship
ordinary	occasion
original	opportunity

imposition
dispossess
unfortunately
horizontal
modernise
modernisation
remodelled
worshipped
occasional
originality

____

____

1. LOOKING AT plurals

Compound nouns add 's' to the most important word.

e.g. son-in-law — sons-in-law

Write the plural.

a. passer-by ______________
b. maid of honour ______________
c. son-in-law ______________
d. mother-in-law ______________
e. court-martial ______________

Form plurals.

f. class __________ g. beauty __________
h. suffix __________ i. yourself __________
j. guess __________ k. climax __________
l. injury __________ m. kidney __________
n. thief __________ o. hanger-on __________
p. hero __________ q. woman __________

Rewrite in the plural.

r. There was a blue butterfly on the branch of the small bush near the fence.

____

____

____

2. Direct & Indirect Speech

Write in direct speech.

a. Mother told Jane to put down her toys as it was her turn to do the washing-up.

____

____

____

b. Mum stammered as she searched for the candles we've blown a fuse.

____

____

____

Write in indirect speech.

c. The lifesaver warned, "Swim between the flags."

____

____

d. Jane cried, "I've lost my way home."

____

____

3. WORD STUDY

Add prefixes and suffixes.

a. _____fortune b. _____fortunate
c. original_____ d. modern_____
e. _____possess f. _____ship_____

Write four words beginning with 'home'

g. __________ __________
__________ __________

Write the three parts of these verbs.

h. modernise __________
__________ __________

i. worship __________
__________ __________

PART 3

The Spirit in the Tree

After the speech the crowd hoped that the tree spirit would convince the king to abandon his plans.

The ordinary people were in no position to alter the king's mind. Only a supreme power could solve the problem.

One afternoon the king was sitting on the balcony of the palace. From here he could see across the forests to the horizon. The king watched in amazement as a golden glow on the horizon began moving towards him, and soon enveloped the balcony.

He heard a deep voice, "Hear me, O king. I am the spirit of the giant tree that has saved this fortunate town from disease and destruction. It is time to save my tree."

The king realised the foolishness of his plan and decided that the tree should be left untouched forever.

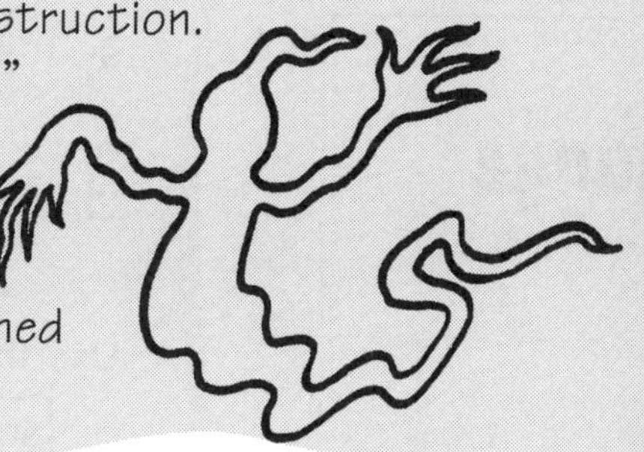

4. word usage

Choose list and extension words.

a. The __________ sound of birds broke the silence.

b. She thought she would have the __________ to win.

c. The members of the family __________ in the local church.

5. Dictionary Work

a. leaning to one side lop__________

b. a poisonous substance nic__________

c. a request in writing pet__________

d. to dry up eva__________

e. a bunch of flowers bo__________

6. CORNER Challenge

Explain these foreign words and phrases.

a. ad lib

____

____

b. bon voyage

____

____

c. debut

____

____

d. et cetera

____

____

e. vice versa

____

____

7. Select-A-WORD

Choose antonyms from the list.

a. antique __________

b. reproduction __________

c. special __________

Add adjectives.

d. __________ homestead

e. __________ occasion

f. __________ position

Analogies. Canberra is to Australia as Ottawa is to __________.

UNIT 29 Extension

attract	tractor
contract	extract
subtract	porter
export	import
support	portable
transport	fluid
fluent	influence

unattractively
distraction
contractor
extraction
portfolio
importance
portability
transportation
transplanted
influential
____
____

1. LOOKING AT language

These words have Latin roots.

'traho' means 'to draw'.

Choose list words.

a. that which draws farm implements __________

b. to draw together an agreement __________

c. to take out __________

d. minus __________

'porto' means 'I carry'.

Explain these words.

e. portable ____________________

f. import ____________________

'fluo' means 'I flow'.

Choose list words.

g. flows in liquid form __________

h. to have 'flowing' language skills __________

Add any of the above Latin roots.

i. super______us

j. im______ant

k. in_____ence

l. at_______ion

2. WORD STUDY

Break these words into syllables.

e.g. slov/en/ly
cir/cum/nav/i/gate

a. transportation

b. portability

c. contractor

The prefix 'trans' means 'across'.
Match words to meanings.

d. thing that crosses another

e. change into another language

f. make copy of

g. hand over

translate
transcribe
traverse
transfer

3. Using Extension Words

Use the pairs of words in sentences.

a. | support | export |

____
____
____

b. | contract | transport |

____
____
____

4. Proof Reading

Add apostrophes where required.

a. The porters driving licence didnt allow him to drive tractors.

b. Im hopeful that we can build an export market.

c. Theyre going to buy Katys car.

BOOK REVIEW

Title: Island of the Blue Dolphin
Author: Scott O'Dell
Review by: Natasha Kassebian
Plot: An Indian girl, named Karana, lived on an island off the coast of California. Her survival, for fifteen years, alone, was a great feat of endurance.
Setting: Sea otters attracted hunters to the island. Karana's family and friends were taken off the island or killed.
Interesting Events: Karana let nothing distract her from surviving. She often had to battle wild animals. Using portable primitive cooking equipment she managed to support herself. Karana tamed a wild dog to be her only companion.
Conclusion: Even a short extract from this book is interesting. It is the best book I have read this year.

6. CORNER Challenge

Explain these words.

a. ultrasonic ____________

b. isotopes ____________

c. fissionable ____________

d. fallout ____________

Find three synonyms for each.

e. umpire ______ ______ ______

f. decorate ______ ______ ______

g. associate ______ ______ ______

5. Adverbial Clauses

Add clauses (remember it must have a verb).

a. Tammy will leave when ____________

b. All the customers will go where ____________

c. He cannot do it because ____________

Use these adverbial clauses in sentences.

d. lest he damage the vase ____________

e. when the new car arrived ____________

7. ABBREVIATIONS

Write in full.

a. Ltd ______ b. perm. ______

c. Pty ______ d. dist. ______

Write the abbreviation.

e. maximum ______ f. establish ______

g. ante meridian ______

h. approximately ______

8. Select-A-WORD

a. The country will ______ new cars when its own factories close. (import, export)

b. Having so much arable land the country could ______ large amounts of grain. (export, import)

Idiom. Explain 'She only eats like a bird' ____________

UNIT 30 Extension

educate	employ
enormous	entertain
entrance	economic
electric	enquiry
erosion	exercise
environment	electorate
experiment	envelope

educational
unemployment
uneconomic
electricity
erode
electoral
enveloping
experimental
inexperienced
environs
____
____

1. LOOKING AT contractions

Write the contractions.

a. who have __________ b. you are __________

c. did not __________ d. who is __________

Write in full.

e. I'm sorry but the car (won't) __________ __________ start.

f. You (aren't) __________ __________ allowed to climb the big tree.

g. I'm sure that telling lies (doesn't) __________ __________ help.

Add the missing apostrophes.

h. were __________ i. youll __________

j. its __________ k. shant __________

Use in interesting sentences.

l. who've ______________________________
____

m. we're ______________________________
____

2. WORD STUDY

Write the nouns as verbs.

a. The company knew it had to (electricity)__________ the line.

b. The puppet show was to (entertainment)__________ the children.

c. Because of declining sales the owner had to (economy) __________.

d. The huge waves will (erosion) __________ the dunes.

e. My young brother was (electorate)__________ to parliament.

3. word usage

Add suffixes.

a. All of the entertain______ was enjoyed by the people.

b. Because the electric______ didn't finish the work, he will return tomorrow.

c. The children who were exercis______ in the playground were in year 6.

d. They went to the employ______ office at nine o'clock.

e. The business operator is the employ______ of a hundred workers.

f. There have been many changes to the educat______ system.

The Mine

The area is enormous. Dust rolls across the entrance, coating machines in fine dust. People emerge enveloped in the powdery grains which enter noses, eyes, ears and throats.

The noise is constant and deafening. It moves in waves from the cliff face enveloping the area in a barrage of sound.

The work appears to be never ending. Many are employed, working day or night shifts, digging and clearing, destroying much.

The result is damaging. The vast wilderness is eroded and the environment altered for ever. Such is progress.

5. CORNER Challenge

Complete the OON words.

a. a small group of soldiers ____________

b. a humorous sketch ____________

c. a person of immense wealth ____________

d. a severe storm of wind and rain ____________

Choose extension words.

e. ____________ driver

f. ____________ program

g. ____________ office

h. ____________ business

4. LOOKING AT language

These words derive from Greek roots.

'phono' means 'sound'.
e.g. phonics, telephone, stereophonic, phonetic

'chronos' means 'time'.
e.g. chronometer, chronicle, synchronise, chronic

'pathos' means 'feeling'.
e.g. sympathy, apathy, antipathy, pathetic

Choose from the above words.

a. She spoke to him on the ____________ for thirty minutes.

b. The ____________ sound from the hi-fi was of exceptional quality.

c. They had no ____________ for the man who had gambled away all his money.

d. It was the janitor's job to ____________ all the clocks.

e. The study of sounds in words ____________

f. That which tells the time ____________

6. Select-A-WORD

Choose list words as adjectives.

a. ____________ machinery

b. ____________ railway

c. ____________ changes

7. Vocabulary

Explain these words.

a. bolshevik ____________

b. quinine ____________

c. zeppelin ____________

d. polo ____________

Idiom. Explain: I felt like 'a fish out of water' ____________

UNIT 31 Extension

happiness	laziness
brightness	faithful
pitiful	truthful
plentiful	beautify
purify	terrify
dentist	artist
florist	cyclist

unhappily
brightening
unfaithfulness
pitiless
untruthfully
beautification
beautician
unpurified
terrific
dental

____

____

1. LOOKING AT *alternative words*

List six words to replace 'said'.

e.g. "Come quickly," said Mum.
— <u>ordered</u> Mum

a. ________ ________ ________

________ ________ ________

Write more interesting words than 'said'.

b. "Yes I did commit the crime," ________ the prisoner.

c. "I lost again," ________ the young boy.

d. "Leave it!" ________ the officer.

List six alternatives for 'nice'.

e. ________ ________ ________

________ ________ ________

Replace 'nice' with more interesting words.

e.g. a nice book — an <u>interesting</u> book

f. It was a ________ cake.

g. She wore an ________ dress.

h. Here are the ________ flowers.

i. They had a very ________ meal.

2. WORD STUDY

The suffix 'ist' means 'one who'.

Write words ending with 'ist'.

a. one who writes plays d________

b. one who studies rock sand minerals g________

c. one who plays an organ o________

d. one who sings v________

The suffix 'fy' means 'to make'.

e.g. purify — to make pure

Explain.

e. magnify ________

f. simplify ________

g. beautify ________

Add words ending with suffix 'ful'.

h. The s________ businessman made a lot of money.

i. The p________ injury caused the girl distress.

3. Adverbial Clauses

Add two adverbial clauses to this sentence.

a. When ________ the animal went where ________

Underline the adverbial or adjectival clauses.

b. Jeremy went to bed early, because he had a tiring day.

c. When the storm broke, the children sheltered in the shed.

d. The hermit who lived near the river was always alone.

e. The cyclist, whom he met last week, won the championship.

Poetry

Cinquains

Dentist
Kind, gentle
Dressed in white
Caring for your teeth
Skilful

Florist
Creative, artistic
Beautifying the room
Arranging colours and shapes
Blooming

Diamantes

Cyclist
Straining, training
Pushing, sweating, puffing
Race, track, happiness, money
Resting, waving, coasting
Proud, smiling
Winner

Artist
Colourful, creative
Flaming, surprising, thrilling
Brightness, lightness, beauty, shapes
Sculpting, moulding, developing
Teaching, fascinating
Creator

5. CORNER Challenge

Choose extension list words.

a. The boy stared __________ at the broken window.

b. Though he spoke __________ people wanted to believe him.

c. The __________ water was not fit to drink.

Write words beginning with 'MAN'.

d. a swamp plant
MAN_ _ _ _ _ _

e. to handle things well
MAN_ _ _ _

f. the movement of troops
MAN_ _ _ _ _ _ _ _

4. PUNCTUATION

Write the abbreviated form.

a. Mister ______ b. Professor ______
c. road ______ d. Wednesday ______
e. have not ______ f. she will ______

Add punctuation.

g. have you read the bridge to terabithia yet she asked

h. weve had enough she exclaimed

i. where in europe have you travelled he asked

j. mrs lippa the shopkeeper was stacking the shelves

6. Select-A-WORD

Choose a list word and word of your own.

a. She has always been a __________ __________ friend.

b. The __________ __________ arranged groups of flowers.

c. She will __________ __________ the water before the experiment.

Find synonyms.

d. honest __________

e. contentment __________

f. disinfect __________

Idiom. Explain: I think that job will <u>be a piece of cake</u>. ______________________________

UNIT 32 Extension

dense	sense
ledge	celebrate
fertile	behave
vehicle	enemy
genre	genetic
necessary	jewellery
temperature	miraculous

sensible
sensitive
insensitively
celebration
fertilise
vehicular
necessity
unnecessarily
temperate
jeweller
____
____

1. LOOKING AT punctuation

Add apostrophe of possession.

a. Our brothers house is next door to that mans shed.

b. Many womens gloves were packed in the servants box.

Punctuate these sentences.

c. my thats great exclaimed jason did you make it yourself

____

____

d. yes we can warned the officer and well be back before sunset

____

____

e. eva and maria have done this exclaimed adam

____

____

2. Select-A-WORD

Choose synonyms from the list.

a. foe __________ b. required __________

c. thick __________ d. wisdom __________

3. Phrases & Clauses

Underline the phrases. Draw a double line under the clauses.

e.g. The children ran in a hurry to the shops.
The children ran to the shops, because they were in a hurry.

a. They jumped from the tractor when it stopped.

b. The man in the jacket was very hot.

c. He could not walk any farther because he was tired.

d. The river between the trees was filled with junk.

e. Suzanne borrowed a book because she had nothing to read.

4. WORD STUDY

Write as adjectives.

a. sens_______ b. vehic_______

c. temper_______

Write words using the prefix 'mis'.

d. to put in the wrong place

____

e. to use the wrong way

____

f. to lead to the wrong place

____

g. to say a word the wrong way

____

Write the verb forms.

h. behave __________

__________ __________

i. celebrate __________

__________ __________

Change to adverbs.

j. dense __________

k. necessary __________

AMAZING ESCAPE

Milltown, Wednesday

A young driver made a miraculous escape from his overturned 4WD on rugged Mt Sloan. This happened just minutes before the vehicle crashed two hundred metres down the cliff face.

The driver, Jason Heriquez, lost control of the vehicle on the timber track. His vehicle crashed through the dense scrub to the cliff's edge. There it balanced on a log while the driver was caught by his sleeve. Jason slowly used his pocket knife to cut himself free. As he jumped to the ground, his vehicle started falling.

"I knew it was necessary to climb out quickly as the ledge was close to the front wheels," Jason explained.

Shocked but unhurt, Jason was picked up by a passing motorist on the Mt Sloan – Milltown Road.

6. CORNER Challenge

Complete the crossword puzzle.

a. to stick with
b. to split into smaller pieces
c. to grow rich
d. to make beautiful
e. state of being happy
f. an independent self governing country
g. to mix or be mixed with another liquid
h. to help
i. to talk to or discuss with another
j. to draw or take out of

5. word usage

Use list and extension words.

a. The __________ was held at the town hall.

b. They took their car across on the __________ ferry.

c. The farmers will __________ the crops this week.

d. She did not think that it was __________ to stay overnight.

e. These crops grow very well in a __________ climate.

f. It was difficult to cut a path through the __________ scrub.

7. Proof Reading

Rewrite incorrectly spelt words.

bandege vehicel harbor economec
causel libary puncture suficient
influence scientist immediate excelent
marvelous manufactere underweight

____

____

____

____

Idiom. Explain: He really is in a stew. ____________________________________

REVIEW

Term 4

1. Choose the word that fits.

dissolve
necessary
electorate
achievement
original
diagram
fluent

a. Climbing a high mountain in difficult weather conditions was a great ___________.
b. The ___________ she drew was accurate.
c. This chemical will ___________ that substance easily.
d. The girl was ___________ in Japanese.
e. They found it was ___________ to collect the books early.
f. The ___________ painting was sold at auction.
g. The people in the ___________ voted last weekend.

2. Change these words to nouns by adding suitable endings.

a. transport ___________
b. necessary ___________
c. original ___________
d. advertise ___________
e. possess ___________
f. electric ___________

3. Change these words to adjectives by adding suitable endings

a. dentist ___________
b. pity ___________
c. divide ___________
d. attract ___________
e. occasion ___________
f. electric ___________

4. Underline and rewrite incorrectly spelt words.

a. The travellar had numeros trips to the capital citys. ___________
b. On this occasion it was a good opportunety to visit the mountains. ___________
c. Unfortunatly he had used varios types of equiptment but none was sucessfull. ___________
d. The vehicel had traveled along the old homested road. ___________

5. Rewrite the sentences correctly.

a. Meny of them had bean their for severl months.

b. Tomorow they will spred the soil on the garden.

c. The lighting flashed in the cloudey sky larst night.

d. The matereal was in the middel of the tabel.

e. She will remane hear until the wrest of them arive.

6. Write words which mean the following. The prefix or suffix clue is provided.

a. state of being an owner ____________ (ship)

b. to sail right around ____________ (circum)

c. a measure through the centre of a circle ____________ (dia)

d. to talk about a particular subject ____________ (dis)

e. to pay beneath the normal amount ____________ (under)

7. Write these words in the plural form.

a. prefix ____________ c. louse ____________ e. son-in-law ____________

b. thief ____________ d. dingo ____________ f. jockey ____________

8. Write word families for these words. You should write at least 6 words for each.

a. agree

b. laze

9. Write synonyms for these words.

a. disagreement ____________ c. entertainment ____________

b. supplies ____________ d. hardship ____________

10. Use these words correctly in sentences.

threw	through

Year 6 DICTIONARY

A a

Aborigine *(noun)* original inhabitants of Australia
accept *(verb)* consent
accessible *(adjective)* able to be reached
accident *(noun)* unlucky event
accommodate *(verb)* adapt
accompany *(verb)* go with
achievement *(noun)* accomplishment
activity *(noun)* state of doing
advertise *(verb)* draw attention to
advertisement *(noun)* public announcement
advice *(noun)* information given
affection *(noun)* goodwill
agreement *(noun)* harmony
agriculture *(noun)* farming
airport *(noun)* where planes land & take off
allowance *(noun)* take into consideration / money for special purpose
ancestor *(noun)* someone you are descended from
ankle *(noun)* joint connecting foot with leg
announcer *(noun)* person who makes something publicly known
antagonist *(noun)* opponent
antidote *(noun)* medicine that counteracts toxins
antiseptic *(noun)* chemical used to kill germs
anxious *(adjective)* worried
appeared *(verb)* came into view
apply *(verb)* to bring into contact with
argument *(noun)* reasons for doing something
article *(noun)* a particular thing
artist *(noun)* someone who practises one of the fine arts
ascent *(noun)* upwards movement
assembly *(noun)* group
assistance *(noun)* help
assistant *(noun)* person whose job is to help another
astrology *(noun)* study of the occult influences of the planets on people's lives
astronomy *(noun)* scientific study of heavenly bodies
attendance *(noun)* being present at
attendant *(noun)* accompanying
attention *(noun)* take notice
attract *(verb)* draw attention
attraction *(noun)* pull towards
audience *(noun)* group of spectators
autograph *(noun)* a famous person's signature

B b

bandage *(noun)* strip of material for binding a wound
battle *(noun)* big fight
beautify *(verb)* to make beautiful
beginning *(verb)* starting
behave *(verb)* to act
behaviour *(noun)* the way someone acts
belief *(noun)* faith
biography *(noun)* someone's life story
biology *(noun)* science of life
bitumen *(noun)* tar
blood *(noun)* red fluid that flows around inside animals' bodies
boarder *(noun)* someone who pays to sleep & eat at someone else's house
border *(noun)* edge
bore *(verb)* make a round hole
borrow *(verb)* have temporary use
boundary (noun) dividing line
breathe *(verb)* to draw breath into the lungs & expel it

brightness *(noun)* how much something shines
brilliant *(adjective)* bright
budget *(noun)* plan of how money will be spent
built *(verb)* made by joining parts together
burglar *(noun)* person who steals things

Cc

calculator *(noun)* device that does maths mechanically
calendar *(noun)* chart of days, weeks & months of the year
cancel *(verb)* call off
candidate *(noun)* one who seeks a position
carriage *(noun)* wheeled vehicle for people
cautious *(adjective)* careful
celebrate *(verb)* engage in festivities
chamber *(noun)* room
champion *(noun)* best at something
chance *(noun)* absence of design
character *(noun)* person portrayed in a book
cheque *(noun)* written order on a bank
choir *(noun)* group who sing together
circumference *(noun)* distance around a circle
circumstances *(noun)* conditions
classify *(verb)* arrange in classes
colony *(noun)* place where people from another country settle
comfortable *(adjective)* at ease
competition *(noun)* test against each other
construct *(verb)* build
contract *(noun)* legal agreement *(verb)* get smaller
contradict *(verb)* disagree
conversation *(noun)* people talking to each other
co-operate *(verb)* work together
correct *(verb)* set right
cough *(verb)* expel air from lungs to remove obstruction
council *(noun)* assembly of people for a purpose
counterfeit *(adjective)* imitation
courage *(noun)* strength of will
culture *(noun)* state of civilization
curious *(adjective)* inquisitive
curtain *(noun)* cloth screen
customer *(noun)* one who buys
cyclist *(noun)* someone who rides a bike

Dd

dairy *(noun)* where cows are milked
defence *(noun)* protection
definite *(adjective)* clearly stated
dense *(adjective)* thick
dentist *(noun)* someone who treats diseases of the teeth
desire *(verb)* to want
dessert *(noun)* sweet course of meal
determine *(verb)* decide
diagonal *(adjective)* straight line joining two non-adjacent angles
diagram *(noun)* drawing that shows how something works
dialogue *(noun)* conversation
diameter *(noun)* straight line
direction *(noun)* point towards which something is moving
disappointed (verb) failed
disease *(noun)* illness
dissolve *(verb)* to disperse

distant *(adjective)* a long way away
distract *(verb)* draw attention away from
divide *(verb)* to separate
drawer *(noun)* receptacle sliding in & out of a frame

Ee

economic *(adjective)* does not cost too much
educate *(verb)* instruct
electorate *(noun)* body of electors
electric *(adjective)* suddenly exciting / using electricity
emperor *(noun)* sovereign
employ *(verb)* use services of a person
employed *(verb)* past tense of employ
endurance *(noun)* withstanding prolonged strain
enemy *(noun)* opponent
enormous *(adjective)* very big
enquiry *(noun)* question, investigation
entertain *(verb)* to amuse
entrance *(verb)* to delight
(noun) way in
envelope *(noun)* covering
environment *(noun)* surroundings
equipment *(noun)* what is needed to do something
erosion *(noun)* worn away
especially *(adverb)* particularly
eventually *(adverb)* at last
examine *(verb)* look carefully
exceed *(verb)* go beyond
excellent *(adjective)* very good
excessive *(adjective)* over the limit
executive *(noun)* manager
exercise *(noun)* activity
exhaust *(verb)* wear out
exhibition *(noun)* display
experience *(noun)* what happens to a person
experiment *(verb)* test
export *(verb)* send to another country
expose *(verb)* uncover
extinct *(adjective)* no longer in existence
extract *(verb)* pull out

Ff

faithful *(adjective)* loyal
fertile *(adjective)* productive
fiction *(noun)* invented story
figure *(noun)* symbol for a number
flavour *(noun)* taste
flight *(noun)* act of flying
florist *(noun)* someone who sells flowers
fluent *(adjective)* speaking easily
fluid *(noun)* liquid
foreign *(adjective)* alien
forth *(adverb)* forward
fortunate *(adjective)* lucky
friendship *(noun)* being friends
furious *(adjective)* raging

Gg

gaze *(verb)* to look steadily
genetic *(adjective)* having characteristics passed from parents to offspring
genre *(noun)* style
geography *(noun)* study of the earth
geology *(noun)* study of rocks
geometry *(noun)* science of lines, surfaces & solids in space
government *(noun)* elected representatives of the people who rule politically

governor *(noun)* one who rules
graphic *(adjective)* vivid / shown with pictures
groceries *(noun)* household goods (flour, sugar, tea etc.)
guidance *(noun)* showing how
guide *(verb)* show the way
guilt *(noun)* violation of moral or penal law

Hh

habit *(noun)* something done regularly
happiness *(noun)* contentment
harbour *(noun)* protected bay where ships can tie up
hardship *(noun)* suffering
horizon *(noun)* where the earth & sky meet
harvest *(noun)* gathering of crops
haste *(noun)* hurry
heaven *(noun)* sky
homestead *(noun)* main house on a big farm
honour *(noun)* esteem
horrible *(adjective)* dreadful
human *(noun)* men & women
humour *(noun)* amusement
humourous *(adjective)* amusing

I i

ignorance *(noun)* not knowing
imaginary *(adjective)* existing only in the imagination
imagine *(verb)* picture in the mind
immediate *(adjective)* without delay
import *(verb)* introduce from another country
impossible *(adjective)* cannot be or be done
improvement *(noun)* made better
incident *(noun)* event
independent *(adjective)* not dependent on others
influence *(noun)* power that affects someone else
inhabitant *(noun)* resident of a place
instruct *(verb)* teach
instrument *(noun)* implement
intercept *(verb)* stop something on its way from one place to another
interesting *(adjective)* holding the attention
interfere *(verb)* intervene
interrupt *(verb)* break into someone else's speech
interview *(noun)* face to face meeting where questions are asked
introduction *(noun)* making known for the first time
investigate *(verb)* examine
invisible *(adjective)* cannot be seen

J j

jail *(noun)* prison
jealous *(adjective)* envious
jewellery *(noun)* jewels worn as adornment
judgement *(noun)* conclusion
juicy *(adjective)* full of juice

Kk

kneel *(verb)* rest the body on the knees
knelt *(verb)* past tense of kneel
knowledge *(noun)* what is known

Ll

labour *(noun)* work
laziness *(noun)* not liking effort
ledge *(noun)* flat narrow shelf
leisure *(noun)* free time
library *(noun)* building containing books that can be borrowed
liquid *(adjective)* flowing like water

Mm

machinery *(noun)* group of machines
magnificent *(adjective)* grand
majority *(noun)* more than half
manual *(adjective)* done by hand
(noun) book on how something works
manufacture *(verb)* make things on a large scale
manuscript *(noun)* copy of book before printing
married *(verb)* joined to another
marvellous *(adjective)* wonderful
masculine *(adjective)* having male characteristics
mathematics *(noun)* science of numbers
maximum *(noun)* greatest number possible
mayor *(noun)* head of a municipal council
meanwhile *(adverb)* at the same time
media *(noun)* (plural of noun medium) means of communication (TV, radio, newspapers & magazines)
messenger *(noun)* person who carries a message
meteor *(noun)* rocks from outer space which enter earth's atmosphere
microbe *(noun)* minute living organism
microscope *(noun)* instrument that magnifies
minimum *(noun)* smallest number possible
minister *(noun)* clergyman / head of government department
miserable *(adjective)* unhappy
mobile *(adjective)* movable
modern *(adjective)* of recent times
mosquito *(noun)* blood sucking insect
musician *(noun)* person skilled in the practice of music
mysterious *(adjective)* puzzling

Nn

necessary *(adjective)* required
neighbour *(noun)* someone who lives close to you
nuclear *(adjective)* relating to a nucleus
numerous *(adjective)* many

Oo

obstruct *(verb)* close off
occasion *(noun)* event
occasionally *(adverb)* sometimes
occupation *(noun)* employment
occupy *(verb)* take possession of
occurred *(verb)* happened
operation *(noun)* the way something works / surgical treatment
opportunity *(noun)* good time / chance
opposition *(noun)* resistance
ordinary *(adjective)* usual
original *(adjective)* first
outcast *(noun)* person outside society
outlaw *(noun)* person outside the law
outlive *(verb)* live longer than
outrun *(verb)* outstrip other runners
overhead *(adverb)* above

P p

palace *(noun)* grand home of important person
panic *(noun)* infectious fright
paragraph *(noun)* distinct section of writing, begun on a new line
parallel *(adjective)* running in the same direction
parcel *(noun)* wrapped bundle
parliament *(noun)* where the government meets
particular *(adjective)* singular
pastime *(noun)* recreation
pastures *(noun)* fields
patient *(noun)* person receiving medical care *(adjective)* waiting quietly
percentage *(noun)* rate per hundred
perimeter *(noun)* outside edge
periscope *(noun)* tube with mirrors used to see from a submerged position or back of a crowd
permanent *(adjective)* lasting
permission *(noun)* allowing something to happen
persist *(verb)* continue obstinately
personal *(adjective)* one's own
persuade *(verb)* convince someone of something
pitiful *(adjective)* helpless
planet *(noun)* heavenly body revolving around the sun
plaster *(noun)* mixture of lime, sand & water
plastic *(adjective)* capable of being easily moulded *(noun)* a soft, man-made material
platform *(noun)* raised area
pleasure *(noun)* enjoyment
plentiful *(adjective)* lots
populate *(verb)* inhabit
population *(noun)* total number of people who live in a place
portable *(adjective)* easily moved
porter *(noun)* someone who carries things
position *(noun)* location
possess *(verb)* to have
possible *(adjective)* that can be done, be or happen
principal *(adjective)* first in importance
principle *(noun)* general rule
probably *(adverb)* likely
procession *(noun)* parade
profit *(noun)* advantage
program *(noun)* list of a series of events
prologue *(noun)* introduction
property *(noun)* something owned
prophecy *(noun)* what will happen in the future
prosperous *(adjective)* wealthy
protection *(noun)* keeping from harm
provide *(verb)* supply
public *(noun)* people as a whole
publication *(noun)* something printed
publisher *(noun)* person responsible for having something printed in multiple copies
puncture *(verb)* prick
purchase *(verb)* buy
purify *(verb)* to make pure
purpose (noun) thing intended

Q q

quality *(noun)* degree of excellence / feature
quantity *(noun)* amount
quarrel *(noun)* complaint

R r

realise *(verb)* understand
receipt *(noun)* note of something received
receive *(verb)* accept
recent *(adjective)* lately
recipe *(noun)* instructions on how to make something
recognise *(verb)* know again
recommend *(verb)* suggest
record *(verb)* put in writing / to put music on a disc or tape
recover *(verb)* regain
rectangular *(adjective)* shaped like a rectangle
refreshment *(noun)* food & drink
regard *(noun)* attention
regular *(adjective)* consistent
replied *(verb)* answered
represent *(verb)* stand for / portray
republic *(noun)* nation with an elected leader
rescue *(verb)* save
restaurant *(noun)* public place for buying & eating meals
revenue *(noun)* income
rifle *(noun)* gun with a long barrel fired from the shoulder
rocket *(noun)* cylinder full of gunpowder fired into the air
ruin *(verb)* destroy

S s

savage *(adjective)* untamed
science *(noun)* systematic knowledge
scientist *(noun)* person with knowledge of science
scramble *(verb)* move over rough ground / mix up
secret *(adjective)* private
secretary *(noun)* someone whose job is to attend to correspondence & records for someone else
section *(noun)* part
seize *(verb)* to take by force
select *(verb)* choose
senator *(noun)* member of the senate
sense *(noun)* meaning
sentence *(noun)* set of words complete in itself / punishment imposed by law court
serious *(adjective)* responsible
service *(noun)* helpful activity
several *(adjective)* not many / separate
shadow *(noun)* shade
shrub *(noun)* a bush
sign *(noun)* written mark
silence *(noun)* absence of sound
silent *(adjective)* making no sound
similar *(adjective)* like
simple *(adjective)* not complicated
sincerely *(adverb)* expressing true feelings
soak *(verb)* leave in liquid for a long time
solar *(adjective)* concerned with the sun
soldier *(noun)* person in the army
special *(adjective)* distinct
spectator *(noun)* person who watches an event
split *(verb)* separate
spoil *(verb)* damage
spoken *(verb)* talked
sprang *(verb)* leaped
square *(noun)* shape with 4 equal sides
startle *(verb)* to suddenly alarm
stationary *(adjective)* still
stationery *(noun)* writing materials

steady *(adjective)* constant
stomach *(noun)* internal organ where food is digested
structure *(noun)* something built
substance *(noun)* matter
subtract *(verb)* take away
succeed *(verb)* accomplish one's purpose
suffer *(verb)* feel pain
sufficient *(adjective)* enough
suitable *(adjective)* appropriate
support *(verb)* keep from falling
surprise *(verb)* do something unexpectedly
survivor *(noun)* one who is still alive
sword *(noun)* weapon with a long blade

T t

telescope *(noun)* tube with powerful lenses that make distant objects seem closer & larger
temperature *(noun)* measure of hot or cold
terrify *(verb)* frighten
theatre *(noun)* place for dramatic performances
therefore *(conjunction)* as a result
thoroughly *(adverb)* completely
tight *(adjective)* closely fitting
tongue *(noun)* fleshy, muscular organ in the mouth
tourist *(noun)* a person who travels for pleasure
towel *(noun)* absorbent cloth
tractor *(noun)* engine for hauling
transport *(verb)* convey from one place to another
traveller *(noun)* person on a journey
truthful *(adjective)* honest
twist *(verb)* combine by winding strands together

U u

unconscious *(adjective)* unaware
underground *(adjective)* beneath the surface of the earth
undermine *(verb)* wear away the foundations of
underpay *(verb)* not pay enough
underweight *(adjective)* weighing less than normal
underworld *(noun)* people living outside the law
unfortunately *(adverb)* unluckily
unhealthy *(adjective)* dangerous
unique *(adjective)* remarkable
untidy *(adjective)* not neat
unusual *(adjective)* out of the ordinary
useable *(adjective)* able to be used

V v

vacuum *(noun)* empty space
valuable *(adjective)* worth a lot
variety *(noun)* diversity
various *(adjective)* diverse
vast *(adjective)* very big
vehicle *(noun)* form of transport
vicious *(adjective)* very cruel

worship *(noun)* reverent homage

youth *(noun)* young people

Year 6 SPELLING RULES

Plurals

1. Usually add **-s** to form the plurals.
   e.g. ice-cream — ice-creams
   Words ending in **s**, **z**, **x**, **ch**, **sh** add **-es**.
   e.g. crunch — crunches

2. Words ending in **consonant-y**, change the **y** to **i** and add **-es**.
   e.g. dictionary — dictionaries

3. Words ending in a **vowel-y** add **-s**.
   e.g. *donkey — donkeys*

4. Usually when a word ends with **f** change the **f** to **v** and add **-es**.
   e.g. yourself — yourselves

5. Some nouns have the **same spelling** whether **singular** or **plural**.
   e.g. salmon, sheep

6. Some plurals **change** the **base** word.
   e.g. mouse — mice

7. Most **singular** words ending in **o** add **-es**.
   e.g. tomato — tomatoes

8. If there is a **vowel before the o** add **-s**.
   e.g. radio — radios

9. **Compound nouns** add **-s** to the most important word.
   e.g. son-in-law — sons-in-law
   passer-by — passers-by

Compound verbs consist of an **auxiliary** and a **main** verb.
She **had simplified** the work.
Had — auxiliary simplified — main

Verbs can be written in different tenses.
I **spoil** the children. (present tense)
I **spoilt** the children. (past tense)
I **have spoilt** the children. (past participle)
I **am spoiling** the children. (present participle)

Verbs can be **active** or **passive**.
Karen visited the zoo. (active)
The zoo was visited by Karen. (passive)

Word building

A **suffix** is a syllable added to the **end** of a word.
e.g. robust + ness = robustness

Simply add suffixes beginning with a **consonant**.
e.g. humourous + ly = humorously
strange + ly = strangely

Words ending in **e**, drop the final **e** when a suffix is added.
e.g. contribute + ion = contribution

Words ending with **ce** or **ge** keep the **e** when adding **able** or **ible**.
e.g. manage + able = manageable

Words ending with **y** change **y** to **i** when adding a suffix.
e.g. weary + ness = weariness

When adding the suffix **full**, **drop the last l**.
e.g. wonder + full = wonderful

When a word ends with a **vowel** and an **l**, the **l** is doubled when a suffix is added.
e.g. model + ed = modelled

If a word ends in **y** this letter is changed to **i** before suffix **ly** is added.
e.g. merry + ly = merrily

A **Prefix** is a syllable added to the **beginning** of a word.
e.g. in + correct = incorrect

Prefixes **sub**, **suc**, **sup**, **sug**, **sus** mean **under**.
e.g. suppress, suspend
Prefix **inter** means **between**.
e.g. interrupt
Prefixes **dis**, **dif**, **di** mean **away** or **apart**.
e.g. distract
Prefixes **in**, **un**, **il** or **ir** mean **not** or the **opposite**.
e.g. legal — illegal
Prefix **ion** means **the act of**.
e.g. affection, extension
Prefix **pro** means **forth** or **forward**.
e.g. proceed